# TRADITIONAL INDIAN COOKING

# TRADITIONAL INDIAN COOKING

## RAMOLA PARBHOO

NEW HOLLAND

*To Pradeep, my husband and soulmate who inspired me since the initial idea to the culmination of this book.*
*To my late dear mother, who taught me most of what I know; to my late father, Thakor Fakir Dullabh,*
*known to all his friends as Delbro, who inspired the initial enthusiasm. To my three daughters, Anita,*
*Lavina and Shakila, in the hope that they—and all other daughters—will keep the tradition of Indian cooking alive.*
*To my three sisters, Sumitra, Indira and Prashilla and all my sisters from here and abroad who have continually*
*shared their culinary delights and spicy secrets with me.*

First published in 1985 by Don Nelson as Ramola Parbhoo's
Indian Cookery for South Africa
Revised and updated edition published in 2008
by Struik Publishers (a division of New Holland Publishing
(South Africa) (Pty) Ltd)

This edition published in Australia in 2012 by
New Holland Publishers (Australia) Pty Ltd
Sydney • Auckland • London • Cape Town

www.newhollandpublishers.com

Garfield House 86-88 Edgware Road London W2 2EA United Kingdom
1/66 Gibbes Street Chatswood NSW 2067 Australia
Wembley Square First Floor Solan Road Gardens Cape Town 8001 South Africa
218 Lake Road Northcote Auckland New Zealand

A copy of this book is held at the National Library of Australia.

ISBN 9781742573717 (pbk)

Publisher: Fiona Schultz
Publishing manager: Lliane Clarke
Project editors: Christine Chua and Joanna Tovia
Designer: Hayley Norman
Production manager: Linda Bottari
Printer: Toppan Leefung Printing Ltd (China)

# Contents

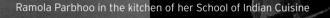

Ramola Parbhoo in the kitchen of her School of Indian Cuisine

# INTRODUCTION

## ACKNOWLEDGEMENTS

My heartfelt thanks to all who have contributed in any way to make this book a wealth of recipes: to all my friends and family who urged me to write and record this knowledge; to Linda de Villiers of Struik Publishers who presented the opportunity for me to revisit my first book, *Indian Cookery for South Africa* and reveal it in this brand new edition; to the original designer Helen Henn and editor Cecilia Barfield; as well as to food photographer Christoph Heierli and stylist Justine Kiggen.

## OUR SCHOOL OF INDIAN CUISINE

Way back in 1980, a vagaar (an aroma) of freshly tempered cumin, fresh curry leaves and ghee drifting through the village of Little Chelsea in Wynberg, Cape Town, altered the path of my career.

Soon this aroma brought my vegetarian neighbour, Sandy, knocking at my door. Sandy was a schoolteacher who taught my three young daughters at the nearby Springfield Convent. The pure delight on her face as she tasted a humble dish of lentils with a piping hot chapati confirmed my new way of life. I was to be a teacher of spices, oriental tastes and the revealer of the magic secrets of basic northern Indian, essentially Gujerati, cooking.

At that time, northern Indian cooking was unknown in South Africa. Very hot curries from southern India were introduced in the late 1800s by the indentured Indians who came to work the sugar cane fields of the then colony of Natal. The very popular curry and rice and bunny chow were typical of South African Indian food.

However, the aromatic and gentler dishes of the north began to capture another audience looking for healthy vegetarian dishes that feature far less heat and spices. My school aimed to fill that gap.

With much encouragement from Sandy and three other neighbours, I launched my very first cookery course from a small area of my dining room. They will never know how that day changed the outlook and course of my life. On their first day I handed them a soft-covered booklet in which I had compiled the recipes to be used on the course. I started with a two-plate, electric plug-in stove, bought for forty rands—a princely sum in those days! With my three young daughters watching wide-eyed and gleefully from the steps, and often sampling the dishes, I started my small home business.

As I cooked simple vegetables and lentils to exotic biryanis with spices and herbs, combining techniques with textures and colours and exotic smells, I blissfully nurtured the art of authentic Indian cooking. At the end of the lesson, we would sit quietly in meditation and enjoy a meal together delighting our senses and enhancing the knowledge of the lesson.

As my creativity emerged, I studied the benefits, practised and cooked the meditative way following the guidelines of Vedic cooking. I rejoiced in the vibrant recipes of the festivals used over and over through the centuries. From generation to generation, just as all the traditions were handed down in India, so was the cuisine kept ablaze by the inclusion of sweetmeats to mark various celebrations, an essential part of life for the people of India.

In the early 1900s, as our parents entered South Africa from Gujerat and other Indian states as small tradesmen and skilled workers, they brought with them this wealth and a knowledge of spices. They cultivated many of the Indian green vegetables and herbs such as dhania, methi, patra, paapri, bitter gourd, lady fingers, lemongrass for tea and, most importantly, the holy basil known as the tulsi plant, in their backyards.

## Lentils, Spices and Hand Downs

Recipes were brought from India on the fingertips of our grandparents, handed down from grandmother to mother or as in my case from father and mother to daughter. No doubt elder sisters and sisters-in-law also contributed to my knowledge. Up to this day the exchange of good recipes through the family and larger community still reigns. Indian cooking has embedded itself as an important tradition in the Hindu way of life.

So it came to be that by 1983, I established the first formal school of Indian cookery in South Africa with hundreds of students who followed the same aroma as Sandy did. I felt much like the Pied Piper of Hamelin; countless students were being led my way by the aromas, and to the tune of the Indian sitar! I gave talks and told stories of the folklore and Hindu traditions, highlighting the endless benefits of the medicinal and healing effects of herbs and spices.

The result of the interaction between students from varying backgrounds and professions was that a deeper understanding of our differences emerged. This interaction through the world of food was a breath of fresh air at this period in the history of South Africa. People of different cultures rarely had the opportunity to sit, enjoy a glass of wine and good food or have meaningful discussions with one another in a normal manner.

The walls of the school in Chelsea reverberated with the sound of laughter and expressions of joy, especially when the students tried their hands at making rotis and puris. Competition was rife as they challenged one another to produce a perfect, blown-up roti or puri at their first attempt.

At the end of each course came the highlighted presentation open day when everyone donned Indian turbans and saris and the menus were cooked by the students themselves. Friends and relatives were invited to share in the students new-found way of eating – with their fingers!

As the East and West merged, I had gathered a family of South Africans, who understood and respected each other's differences. Schooling people who shared the love of good food, fun and happiness was my reward, and many of them became my friends for life.

With all the queries from my students and the recipes that I had tried and tested over and over again, the natural culmination of this study and knowledge was the publication of my first cookbook.

## My mother's kitchen

At age six, like most Hindu girls, my mother encouraged me to sit cross-legged on the kitchen floor and play, a round roti board with quaint legs placed in front of me. With a piece of dough in one hand and a dainty Indian rolling pin in the other, I was taught to make roti or chapati, the traditional breads of India. No matter what the shape or colour of the end result, she was always proud of me. Needless to say, I had a highly qualified teacher as my mother had a reputation for being a supreme cook with magic in her fingers. Her endless patience and industry, with a natural flair for combining spices, textures and colours, have always been an inspiration to me.

Her day started at sunrise when the gentle clatter of pots and pans and the aroma of freshly picked citronella grass brewing with spicy tea issued from her kitchen. The sweet, gentle smell of the incense lit after her morning prayers lingered in the background. I would jump out of bed and scurry along to the kitchen to sit near the coal stove and sip the hot, sweet milky tea, which was both nourishing and filling.

I remember the array of gleaming Indian pots, or tapela, arranged in orderly grades according to shape and size on a ledge above the coal stove. Some were made of brass and were highly polished and silvered on the inside to keep the brassy taste out; these my mother had used in India to carry water through the village. They were the pride of her kitchen. On the other side of the kitchen stood rows of jars containing a selection of pulses and lentils—a month's supply or more.

Earthenware pickle jars and pots, iron griddles, karahais, long ladles and rice spoons, were just some of the typical Indian wares decorating our modest kitchen. Here my mother spent a great deal of her time, like most Hindu mothers, going about daily chores that included the preparation of a pile of delicious hot rotis, ready to be served from the hot griddle, straight onto the plates of her hungry family.

Her day only ended when the last drops of warm milk, sometimes boiled with delicious almonds and cardamom, were poured into my cup to ensure a good night's sleep.

## My father's chicken tarkhari

Nostalgically, I remember the Sundays when partaking of a dish of fresh chicken tarkhari was more a family ritual than a meal. Very early on a Sunday morning my father drove to a nearby farm. There he would share a cup of coffee with the farmer and discuss the recent rain and crops. (The farmer, in turn, often came to town and drank Indian tea while he bought his family's clothes from my father's business.)

The farmer slaughtered two of his plumpest chickens for us. As soon as we arrived home, the chickens were immersed in boiling water, to soften the roots of the feathers. Then my mother and I plucked the feathers until the chickens were clean. I will never forget the awful smell of the feathers.

My father cut the chicken into portions and the grand meal commenced. While my elder sisters prepared a pile of fresh rotis, delicious relishes and dhania (coriander) chutney, my mother pounded fresh masalas with a mortar and pestle.

On these days my father reigned supreme over the kitchen. Fathers are often idolised by their daughters, and I was no exception. To watch his culinary creations was a delightful treat in more ways than one. He loved a challenge and had no inhibitions about using spices, traditionally or otherwise. In fact, he delighted in opposing my mother's methods totally, which made the performance even more interesting.

First, he chose the largest tapeli, a flat Indian pot my mother seldom used. It was his belief that a large pot left space above the chicken for the aroma which would soon emanate from his selected spices. The potent and exotic vagaars (aromas from spices) would have the neighbours paying unexpected visits. No doubt they had some hope of sharing his 'curry', as they knew it. Inevitably, that is what happened, as the ingrained Indian trait of generosity was strong in my father.

He would fling whole tomatoes into the tapeli and, not only squeeze out the juice of the lemon, but cook with some of the rind as well. Occasionally, whole mangoes went into the pot. Kesar (saffron) was the only ingredient my father would use for colouring, much to my mother's indignation as he sprinkled her precious and expensive kesar generously over his chicken tarkhari. Fresh herbs, spring onion and mint were other major sources of flavouring.

My mother was not allowed to touch the pot while the meal was being prepared and, above all, she was never permitted to empty the tarkhari from his big pot into a more suitable or smaller one. My father believed that the tarkhari's essence would be lost if it were to be transferred to another container. It had to remain in the tapeli until every morsel was consumed. When the dish was completed, it was presented on a large blue and gold communal platter and served with flaky roti, kachoomer (salad), chutney and a bowl of basmati rice. The family sat around the table, eating from one platter.

Much of the day's entertainment was seeing how this ritual provoked my mother's fiery temperament. Not only had her spouse dominated her entire kitchen, violated every culinary rule that her own mother had taught her, reduced her cherished year's supply of kesar from Kashmir, and increased the pile of dishes in her kitchen sink, but he gained the reputation of a gourmet cook in the eyes of his friends and neighbours. Worst of all, he stole all the admiration of her doting and innocent daughter. This my mother discovered to her dismay when she overheard a conversation. My father had just completed one of his dishes, had given me a taste and asked me if I enjoyed his food. I replied that when I ate my mother's food, I licked my fingers, but when I ate his food, I bit my fingers. The look of triumph on his face will be embedded in my memory forever.

## Are Savoury Recipes A Secret family Legacy?

Sharing a recipe with a sister is like sharing an exciting secret.Discovering little tricks and techniques are how traditional recipes are nurtured in the family treasure box of recipes. I watched my sister Sumitra pull out a drawer hidden under her bed with the help of her 5-year-old grandson, Akshay. From it she retrieved a neatly handwritten recipe book of antiquity and shared with me the knowledge to make a perfect vegetable bake. Better still, her paper-thin poora recipe is exceptional!

And so it is when making moothia and patra the way my mother did. Indira, my second elder sister, mastered my mother's technique by watching her over and over again. Eventually, she developed the art of making melt-in-the-mouth moothia. With just enough crispness on the outside to hold the delicacy together, the buttery yet bitter flavour of fresh methi or fenugreek herbs awakens the tastebuds – an ingenious yet simple savoury with health benefits.

My younger sister, Prashilla, has mastered the art of making exceptional magaj. I'll never forget the day she visited my brother, Subash, in hospital on his dying day. She was just in time to place a piece of magaj, his favourite sweetmeat, in his mouth. What a touching goodbye that was. Prashilla also makes the tastiest khudi imaginable. The ordinary, warm buttermilk gravy is enriched with fresh cream, fresh curry leaves and a special khudi masalo that makes a regular khudi pale into insignificance.

A memory that lingers is the khudi and khitcheri that I once enjoyed in the home of Jubie, my childhood friend, in Rothrist, Switzerland. And could a simple rice dish such as khitcheri feature as an important meal in the heart of Switzerland! Only if the maker has her roots firmly based in Alipur, Gujerat, India, by way of her mother and father. Ismailkaka and Fatimkaki were legendary figures from our past who adopted us as family. The unforgettable aroma of ghee on big, hot rotis over Fatimkaki's coal stove were a treat on regular afternoon visits with my mother. Little girls were tagged along and thus my love for making these tasty rotis developed.

As a young bride, my sister-in-law Lalita lived with my brother, Subash, in our family home. Back in the mid-1960s she perfected the puffiest, round rotis. As a young girl, I practised for hours under her guidance to emulate her technique. I was being groomed for youthful marriage at the age of 18 and needed to prove my credentials. In those days, the family name would be frowned upon if a young bride could not produce a perfect roti or a grilled papadum by the time she entered her mother-in-law's home!

I have such fond memories of my sister-in-law Kanta welcoming us with her warmth and the lightest of home-baked cakes and delicate biscuits when we visited. She, too, had perfected the art of making really good chai, resulting from my brother Jayraj's hourly demands for fresh ginger and lemongrass tea. (He was also quite adept at making his own delicious chai.)

My niece, Mohini, makes mookhoo just like my mother did and is happy to distribute her recipes to all the family. But it was my aunt Kamoomasi who taught me to make perfectly puffed foolka when I was 21, cradling my crying baby Anita on one arm while sitting in her kitchen.

As these recipes are shared among friends and relatives, we are enriched with new ideas and techniques, enlightened by each other's experience. By word of mouth and community life we are able to keep the art of Indian cooking alive, reminding us of a time when recipe books were superfluous.

# REDUCING PRESSURE IN THE KITCHEN

Pressure cookers may seem at odds in a traditional Indian kitchen, but that is one myth I would like to dispel. Many dishes (such as soups) may be simplified, especially if all the lentils, meat and vegetables are cooked in a pressure cooker, as I learnt after many years of resistance to using one.

If he were here today, an old friend and neighbour would be very happy to see me making use of my small, quaint pressure cooker. Old Mr Bhikubhai Vallabh's gift is finally coming into its own. As a 'thank you' gift for all the khudi, khitcheri and bhaji that I used to prepare for him, just before he died he asked his daughter to buy me a pristine, stainless steel pressure cooker.

Even though I thought the shiny Indian-made cooker rather beautiful, I had deep reservations about using it. Years later, I finally put my trepidation aside and plucked up the courage to unpack it. I had been so indoctrinated by my mother, as to the dangers of such a device as I grew up, that I put aside my common sense...until I was seduced by this charming gift.

However, my mother's fear of, and bad experience with a pressure cooker was not unfounded. The accident happened after she had just started cooking a batch of fresh sheep's trotters with lentils and spices. For some reason, the cooker she was using did not release the pressure. Before long, the pot exploded with a catastrophic bang. To our bewilderment, the trotters' curry hit the ceiling of our kitchen!

Thus it took many years for me to welcome a pressure cooker into my kitchen. When I did, my time in the kitchen diminished radically! I finally found time to smell the roses.

# BUYING, STORING AND ROASTING SPICES

A fresh supply of spices never fails to please an Indian cook, since dishes made with really fresh spices always bear a mark of distinction.

Select spices that will be regularly used; buy them in small quantities, approximately 100 g of each. Store the spices in labelled airtight jars, or in Indian spice dishes – the most practical storage containers designed for the Indian cook.

The average lifespan of spices ranges from 6 to 12 months and is largely dependent on the quality and storage of the spices. To test the quality of most spices, crush the seed. If the spice is fresh, it will emit a good aroma. Discard spices that are soft and appear damp.

Whole spices yield the most aroma when roasted. Spices also have a longer shelf life once roasted as all the moisture is removed. Pre-heat the oven to 180°C. Place spices on a tray, then pick them over and sort to remove small, unwanted bits. Spices such as cumin seeds can be placed in a strainer and rinsed through with cold water. Pat them dry with a cloth.

Spread the spices on a baking tray and place on the middle shelf of the oven. Leave for 30 to 60 minutes, stirring occasionally, until the spices emit a strong aroma and are completely dry. Cool, then store in an airtight container or in a stainless steel spice dish.

When recipes call only for small quantities of roasted spices, use a small saucepan and a rice spoon, or an Indian griddle, over a low heat on the stove top. Stir the spices and 'roast' for 2 minutes.

# Metric measures

For convenience, I have, wherever possible given the ingredients not only in metric volumes but also in metric cups (C), tablespoons (T) and teaspoons (t). These additional measures have been based on the following table of approximate equivalent.

However, cookery is an art, not a pedantic science and I have often chosen to give small amounts in teaspoons (in the case of spices) or tablespoons (in the case of cooking oil or melted ghee) since these are the measures I would use myself. Teaspoons are abbreviated to tsp and tablespoons are referred to as tbsp.

### LIQUID

| | | |
|---|---|---|
| 1 litre | (35 fl oz) | 4 cups |
| 750 ml | 26 fl oz) | 3 cups |
| 500 ml | (18 fl oz) | 2 cups |
| 375 ml | (13.2 fl oz) | 1½ cups |
| 250 ml | (9 fl oz) | 1 cup |
| 200 ml | (7 fl oz) | ¾ cup |
| 125 ml | (4 fl oz) | ½ cup |
| 80 ml | (2 1/2 fl oz) | ⅓ cup |
| 60 ml | (2fl oz) | 4 tablespoons/¼ cup |
| 45 ml | (1.5 fl oz) | 3 tablespoons |
| 30 ml | (1fl oz) | 2 tablespoons |
| 15 ml | | 1 tablespoons |
| 20 ml | | 4 teaspoons |
| 10 ml | | 2 teaspoons |
| 8 ml | | 1½ teaspoons |
| 5 ml | | 1 teaspoons |
| 3 ml | | ½ teaspoons |
| 2 ml | | ¼ teaspoons |

### WEIGHT

| | |
|---|---|
| 15 g | ½ oz |
| 30 g | 1 oz |
| 60 g | 2 oz |
| 90 g | 3 oz |
| 220g | 7 oz |
| 250 g | 8 oz |
| 500 g | 1 lb |
| 1 kg | 2.2 lb |

### OVEN TEMPERATURES

| | | |
|---|---|---|
| Moderately slow | 160°C (325°F) | Gas Mark 3 |
| Moderate | 180-190°C (250-375°F) | Gas Mark 4 |
| Moderately hot | 200-210°C (400-425°F) | Gas Mark 5 |

# SPICE LIST

## AJOWAN

### AJMO (AJWAIN)
*Carum copticum*
Celery-like seeds from a tall herb of the family Umbelliferae. Small, brown and striped, the seeds have a pungent, sharp taste.
**In cooking** Used as an aromatic for vegetables such as peas, beans and potatoes, ajowan may also be used as an unusual flavouring for savouries.
**Other uses** Ajowan is a good remedy for flatulence and is used extensively in the East to alleviate colic.

## ANISEED (LARGE)

### SOOMPH (VARYARI)
*Pimpinella anisum*
Small, elongated green seeds with a taste of liquorice.
**In cooking** Roasted and then crushed, the seeds give Indian savouries such as chilli bites an excellent flavour. In southern India they are used to flavour fish and vegetable dishes.
**Other uses** It is customary in an Indian home to hand a small plate of roasted aniseed around after meals. The seeds are also used as a digestive and as a breath freshener.

## ASAFOETIDA

### HING
*Ferula assafoetida*
A reddish-brown dried resin, derived from the roots of various plants from western Kashmir, East India and Iran.
It has a strong, even foetid odour and a garlicky taste.
**In cooking** Because asafoetida is a digestive, it is chiefly used in lentil and bean dishes. I suggest that you buy this spice in powder form at Indian stores, as the gum has to be roasted in the oven and thereafter ground to a fine powder. It is a powerful seasoning that is always used sparingly.
**Other uses** Asafoetida is one of the best remedies for flatulence. It is used in digestive powders and in the East as an antidote for opium.

## CARAWAY

### CARAWAY
*Carum carvi*
Seldom used in Indian cooking. Caraway is often confused with cumin (jeero), although the taste is quite different.

## CARDAMOM PODS

### ELACHI
*Elettaria cardamomum*
The dried fruit of a plant of the ginger family, containing small, black, highly aromatic seeds. The buff-coloured pod is about the size of a large pea and is usually sun dried. The greener pods are oven dried and contain the more aromatic and pungent seeds, which have a lemony flavour.
**In cooking** The seeds in the buff-coloured pods are used in sweet dishes, and are a primary ingredient of gharum masala, the compound spice mixture used as a garnish. Seeds from the green pods are roasted and ground, and used in milk delicacies as well as Indian desserts.
   In the case of main dishes, most of my recipes call for the whole pods. The pods are not meant to be eaten.
**Other uses** Cardamom is used in the East as a breath freshener as well as an appetite stimulant.

## CAYENNE/RED PEPPER
MIRCHA
*Capsicum frutescens*
Hot, pungent chilli sold ready ground.
**In cooking** It is used in meat, fish, poultry and egg dishes as well as soups, sauces and pickles.

## CHILLI
MIRCHA
*Capsicum frutescens*
Red or green pods – about 12 cm long and 3 cm wide – that contain pungent seeds, which impart the sensation of extreme burning.
**In cooking** Chillies are the prime ingredient in masalas, giving dishes their necessary heat and flavour. Fresh, green chillies contain flat, white seeds and have a distinctive flavour. They have considerable vitamin A and C content and are readily available.

The dried red chilli is either used whole in certain dishes to impart a specific aroma, or it is ground to a fine powder known as cayenne pepper or chilli powder.

In some instances the seeds, which are the source of the heat, are removed from the dried red chilli to reduce the heat of a dish.
**Other uses** The medicinal properties of chillies are important in the East. Powdered chillies are used to neutralise poison and numbness of the body, as well as to relieve hypothermia in cases of cholera.

## CINNAMON/CASSIA
TUJ
*Cinnamomum cassia*
The more pungent and rougher-looking cinnamon sticks used in Indian cookery are, in fact, cassia bark, which, when ground, produces a slightly redder powder than true cinnamon, *Cinnamomum zeylanicum*.

Both the cassia (also known as Chinese cinnamon) and cinnamon tree belong to the evergreen laurel family. The finely rolled cinnamon sticks used in Western cooking do not have a strong enough flavour for Indian cuisine.
**In cooking** Cinnamon/cassia is used as an aromatic for meat, chicken, rice, peas, chana lentils and pickles. Ground cinnamon is used for sweet dishes, milk puddings and spicy tea.
**Other uses** Because it is an aromatic, cinnamon/cassia bark may be chewed to freshen the breath. It is also said to strengthen the gums.

## CLOVES
LAVANG
*Eugenia caryophyllata*
Small, dark brown spikes resembling nails, cloves are the dried flower buds of the tropical evergreen clove tree. They contain a highly scented oil.
**In cooking** Cloves are used for their aromatic qualities in meat, chicken and rice dishes. They are also an essential ingredient of gharum masala. Remove before serving.
**Other uses** Clove oil is used as a local anaesthetic. A whole clove may be chewed for temporary relief from toothache and as a breath freshener. Cloves scattered in the linen cupboard keep household insects at bay and linen smelling fresh.

## CORIANDER SEEDS
DHANIA
*Coriandrum sativum*
Round ridged seeds that range from white to yellowish brown and are slightly smaller than peppercorns, harvested from an umbelliferous plant similar to cow parsley.
**In cooking** The seeds are highly aromatic and have a lemony or sage-like flavour. Ground coriander seed is one of the most

important ingredients in the flavouring of any delicately spiced dish, and is used extensively in vegetable and savoury dishes. The coriander herb grown from the seeds is a basic ingredient of all Indian dishes.

**Other uses** Coriander is an aid against flatulence and is also a cooling agent. A paste of ground coriander seed and water applied to the forehead may relieve headaches.

### CUMIN SEEDS
JEERO
*Cuminum cyminum*
Yellowish-brown seeds of a plant that, like parsley and coriander, belongs to the carrot family. They impart a flavour similar to that of caraway.**In cooking** Cumin is an important ingredient in most vegetarian dishes. It is highly aromatic and is used whole in vegetable and lentil dishes. Crushed cumin is an excellent flavouring for fresh chutneys, salads, yoghurt drinks and dressings. It is often combined with two parts of coriander to one part of cumin for Indian vegetarian dishes.

### CURRY LEAVES
LIMRI (KARIYAPULA)
*Chalcas koenigii*
Small, green, lemon-flavoured leaves that impart a characteristic flavour to southern Indian dishes. The fresh leaves may be bought at Indian stores and dried in the sun. Store in an airtight jar.

**In cooking** The pungent leaves are used whole in most dishes requiring their flavour. Fish and potato dishes are particularly enhanced by these leaves, which may also be used with red lentils or oil lentil dishes.

### FENUGREEK SEEDS
METHI
*Trigonella foenum-graecum*
Small, reddish-brown seeds of a plant from the pea family, with a bitter flavour and a strong, sweetish smell reminiscent of burnt sugar.

**In cooking** Lightly roasted seeds are used for their aroma in fish, potato and savoury dishes.

The fenugreek herb is used for its bitter flavour, particularly in savouries, mince and Indian pancakes.

**Other uses** Fenugreek gives relief from coughs, asthma and rheumatism. In India, child-bearing women are expected to drink fenugreek water for back pain, and eat special sweets made with a selection of nuts, jaggery, dill seed and fenugreek.

**Fenugreek water** Soak 15 ml (1 tbsp) fenugreek seed in 125 ml (½ C) warm water overnight. Strain and sweeten with honey. Take daily for 2 weeks to relieve backache.

### MUSTARD SEEDS
RAI
*Brassica nigra*
These are the tiny, reddish-brown seeds of a plant eaten with relish in northern India as a kind of spinach. The seeds are highly nutritious.

**In cooking** Mustard seeds are used in lentil and vegetable dishes. Take care when using them as they tend to explode and splutter oil when heated.

Mustard oil is used in cooking and pickle-making, particularly in Bengal and northern India.

**Other uses** A pinch of mustard powder can increase the appetite and also hastens digestion.

## NUTMEG
## JAIPHUL
*Myristica fragrans*

The evergreen nutmeg tree bears a yellow fruit enclosing a pit or seed that is dried as nutmeg. (The fleshy red network surrounding the seed is dried separately as mace.)

**In cooking** Grated nutmeg is used extensively to flavour milk and sweet dishes. Use whole nutmeg or, alternatively, grate freshly for maximum flavour over vegetables, soups, sauces and puddings.

## PAPRIKA
## PAPRIKA
*Capsicum annum*

Finely ground red powder made from the fruit of several chilli plants. Popular in Spain.

**In cooking** Use in fish dishes.

## PEPPERCORNS, BLACK OR WHITE KARA (DORA) MARI
*Piper nigrum*

Small berries grown on a tropical vine, chiefly in southwestern India. Black pepper is the whole berry picked when green, then sun dried. White pepper, sharper than black, is the core of the ripe berry.

**In cooking** Peppercorns are a principal ingredient in gharum masala, which acts as a hot garnish.

They are also used in pickles and chutneys. Pepper is also used as a garnish, for example in salads, when heat is required.

## SAFFRON
## KESAR
*Crocus sativus*

This is still the most prized and expensive spice from the East, consisting of the dried stigmas of the saffron flower. They grow in cooler climates, for example in the Himalayan foothills.

Harvested by hand, some 75 000 blossoms are needed to produce 500 g of saffron.

**In cooking** A small amount of saffron can colour a large amount of water; it is usually soaked in warm water or milk to extract its brilliant yellow hue.

Saffron also contributes a mildly bitter, honey-like flavour to food and is used in

A colourful array of spices at the market

most of the exotic rice dishes of India, such as biryani, pilau and certain delectable sweet dishes. A few of the dried filaments (approximately half a teaspoon) will impart flavour and colour to an average-sized dish.

It is preferable to buy the threads as opposed to the powder.

### SESAME SEEDS
### TAL
*Sesamum indicum*
These are small, beige, unhulled seeds. They are highly nutritious and have a nutty flavour, especially when roasted. Sesame seeds are used extensively as a health food product in the West.

**In cooking** The seeds are used in many sweets and for flavouring certain vegetable savouries.

Sesame oil, which is extracted from the seed, is a sweet oil used for cooking in certain parts of India.

### TAMARIND
### AAMLI
*Tamarindus indica*
This is the edible brown pulp of the seed pod from a tree cultivated throughout the tropical world.

**In cooking** The dried seed pod is soaked in warm water to extract its acidic watery pulp. The pulp is especially used in southern India, where it is valued for its acidic, yet sweet taste. It is preferable to vinegar when tartness or piquancy is required.

### TURMERIC
### HALUD (ARAD)
*Curcuma longa*
It is the dried fleshy rhizome of a perennial plant belonging to the ginger family. When fresh, the roots, in fact, resemble ginger, but are yellow. It is usually sold ground or fresh.

**In cooking** Turmeric's bright yellow pigment, used for colouring, makes it the principal ingredient in Indian dishes. Like the chilli, it should be respected: it has an earthy, pungent flavour and very strong, woody aroma. It may overwhelm and ruin a dish.

Turmeric is used in ground form, as a powder to colour Indian dishes.

# Special techniques in Indian cooking

## Vagaar

Vagaar means the captured aroma of selected seeds, through a tempering that is an integral process of Indian cooking. A good vagaar is highly important in Indian cooking. A well-prepared dish should have not only the right flavour of spices, masalas and herbs, but the warmth and aroma of spices such as cinnamon, cloves, cardamom and cumin. This is only possible if a good vagaar is created.

**TO MAKE A VAGAAR** When a recipe calls for a vagaar, it simply means that you must heat a small quantity of oil or ghee (clarified butter) to a high temperature in a saucepan. Place your selected seeds in the saucepan, replacing the lid immediately to avoid losing the aroma the heated seeds will emit within a few seconds. Add the basic ingredients of the recipe quickly, once again covering the saucepan immediately to secure the aroma. If you burn your vagaar spices, be sure to start all over again.

## Masala

If you intend developing your knowledge of Indian cooking, avoid using curry powders as they are never used in the true Indian kitchen. The term 'curry' is derived from the Tamil word 'kari', which means stew or sauce and simply cannot represent all the exotic dishes of the East.

Unfortunately, the misconception of the term curry that has been adopted in the West gives the impression that all Indian food contains curry powder, and that the taste invariably has to be similar.

Indian cuisine offers an almost unlimited repertoire of dishes. Learning to make your own masalas is an excellent beginning. The advantage of developing your own range of masalas is that you will quickly obtain the exact taste your dishes require, putting the stamp of individuality on your cooking. Masalas are intended to suit the particular ingredients and techniques of each recipe.

A masala is a powdered mixture of the principal ingredients necessary for any particular dish. It can either be made of fresh ingredients such as chillies, ginger and garlic, or from dried roasted spices.

Though compound spices such as gharum masala or dhania-jeero (coriander-cumin) may be readily purchased at Indian grocers, they cannot match the fragrance and freshness of the homemade product. It is well worth your while to grind the spices from the whole seeds, taking a little time and trouble to obtain the subtle taste and freshness which only home grinding gives to your dishes. Use a blender, processor, mincer, electric food grinder or a simple mortar and pestle to grind masalas.

It is still common practice in India to make a fresh supply of masalas daily. During my recent visit I learned that the average suburban housewife in India enjoys the privilege of domestic help to make her fresh masalas daily, as well as a variety of chutneys and pickles, hot chapati or bread, and in some cases the entire preparation of the meal. Labour is abundant and relatively inexpensive.

The village housewife in India may enjoy a similar privilege, since intinerant spice grinders are among the many hawkers crowding the streets. In fact, groups of women who are professional spice pounders go from house to house carrying their cumbersome equipment. One woman will pound fresh turmeric or masala with a mortar and pestle, while the others grind spices to a powder between massive stone discs. I was fascinated by their deft manipulation of this unsophisticated equipment, and realised that my modern, space-age kitchen gadgets would be almost offensive to these women, who took such pride in producing the smoothest masalas and finest ground spices.

I watched the women crouching with their bright cotton saris draped between their legs as they chatted and contentedly turned the chakki. Many such people earn a pittance, yet India retains the quality of contentment inherent in her people. I realised that the sophistication of the modern world would only rob these women of their natural charm and peace.

Masalas are possibly the most time-consuming part of Indian cooking. But once a good amount has been made, Indian cooking becomes one of the simplest cuisines in the world.

The success of Indian cooking depends largely on the availability of home-ground spices in the kitchen. I suggest six basic mixtures, to be prepared and stored for up to 3 months: red masala; green masala; ginger paste; garlic paste; the coriander-cumin mixture known as dhania-jeero; and gharum masala, a hot garnish of mixed dry spices.

## How to handle chillies

You need to take special care when handling chillies. Their volatile oil can make your skin tingle and your eyes burn. Use a pair of rubber gloves, but avoid touching your face or eyes while working. If you don't wear rubber gloves, try rubbing sunflower oil onto your hands to prevent irritation. Never work with chillies when children are around.

To clean chillies, rinse them in cold water. Hot water causes fumes to rise from dried chillies and these may irritate your eyes and nose. For beginners, it may be advisable to work under cold, running water when removing the stem of the chilli. Rinse chillies several times before use in a masala.

The best type of dried or fresh chillies to use, when making masalas, are the long, thin ones. It is interesting to note that the flavour of the chilli is in the fleshy pod itself, while the seeds are responsible for the heat of the chilli. Whenever a recipe calls for chillies, remember to use both the pods and the seeds.

Masalas give heat to any dish. If you require less heat, reduce the amount of masala as indicated in the recipes. If you need more heat, add a little more masala, but do not increase any other ingredients.

# GREEN MASALA | *LEELO MASALA*

*Use the fresh, long green chillies available from most supermarkets.*

100 g green chillies
40 g fresh garlic cloves
50 g fresh root ginger
15 ml (1 tbsp) sunflower oil
5 ml (1 t) salt
a pinch turmeric

LARGE QUANTITY FOR FREEZING
— ENOUGH FOR 30 DISHES
500 g green chillies
400 g fresh garlic cloves
400 g fresh root ginger
30 ml (2 tbsp) salt
90 ml (6 tbsp) sunflower oil
3 ml (½ t ) turmeric-optional
juice of 1 lemon-to maintain the green
colour of masala

Protect your fingers and wash the chillies, peel the garlic and scrape the skin off the ginger. Add the oil, salt and turmeric, then pound to a paste with a mortar and pestle (the traditional Indian method), or use a food processor, or a small blender or liquidiser: place the chillies, garlic and ginger in the machine. Add the oil so that the machine has some liquid. Process to a fine paste.
**Enough for 10 dishes**

TO STORE

The turmeric, salt and oil mixture acts as a preservative, enabling the masala to be kept for 2 to 8 weeks in the refrigerator. Store in a glass jar with a close- fitting lid.

Freezing any excess is a good way of keeping masalas almost indefinitely. Storing reduces the fresh flavour of chillies, but not their heat. The storing of masalas is convenient for people who have only limited time for cooking.

USES

Besides making food chilli-hot, green masala adds a fresh chilli taste to any dish. Particularly good with fresh vegetables, fish, chicken and egg dishes.

# RED MASALA | *LAL MASALA*

*Red masala is far hotter than green masala.*

100 g dried red chillies
50 g fresh garlic cloves
50 g fresh root ginger
15 ml (1 tbsp) cooking oil
5 ml (1 t) salt
3 ml (½ t) turmeric
45 ml (3 tbsp) water
10 ml (2 t) cooking oil (extra to cover)

LARGE QUANTITY FOR FREEZING
— ENOUGH FOR 30 DISHES
500 g dried red chillies
400 g fresh garlic cloves
400 g fresh root ginger
90 ml (6 tbsp) cooking oil
30 ml (2 tbsp) salt
3 ml (½ t) turmeric

Protect your fingers and follow the same method as for green masala, adding the water to mix.
**Enough for 10 dishes**

TO STORE

Store in a glass jar, covering the masala with 2 t oil.

USES

Red masala imparts an attractive reddish colour and is often used for meat, fish, chicken and lentil dishes.

# HOT GARNISH OF MIXED GROUND SPICES | *GHARUM MASALA*

*A final spicing to enhance meat dishes. Seldom used in the initial stages of any dish.*

10 g elachi (whole cardamom pods), preferably green
10 g tuj (cinnamon sticks)
10 g lavang (whole cloves)
20 g jeero (cumin seeds)
30 g dhania (coriander seeds)
30 g whole black peppercorns

Open the cardamom pods to remove the seeds. Break the cinnamon into small pieces. Roast spices in oven for 30 minutes but do not allow to brown. Grind the spices in a coffee grinder to make a very smooth powder.
**Enough for 24 dishes**

# CORIANDER-CUMIN SPICE MIXTURE | *DHANIA-JEERO*

*An essentially Gujerati spice mixture, used exclusively for vegetarian dishes.*

65 g dhania (coriander seeds)
35 g jeero (cumin seeds)

Follow instructions for roasting spices (page 10). Place the roasted seeds in an electric blender and blend at a high speed for 2 to 3 minutes until they have the texture of coarse powder.
**Enough for 12 dishes**

Garlic masala, green masala, red masala, ginger masala, dhania-jeero, gharum masala

## GARLIC
## LAHSAN
*Allium sativum*
Garlic is an indispensable ingredient in Indian cookery.

**GARLIC PASTE** To make enough for 12 dishes, you need 100 g garlic cloves, 30 ml (2 tbsp) salt and 45 ml (3 tbsp) cooking oil. Garlic gives off a strong oil which may cause a burning sensation. Rub the tips of your fingers with cooking oil to form a barrier.

Soak the cloves of garlic in hot water for 30 minutes, to loosen the skins and make peeling easier.

A quick way to peel garlic is to cut the clove lengthwise on its broader side and then pop the clove out of the skin. Place garlic, salt and oil in a blender and reduce to a paste, or use a mortar and pestle.

**TO STORE PASTE** Keep in a glass, screw-top jar in the refrigerator for up to 8 weeks. The paste may also be frozen for up to 6 months.

## ROOT GINGER (FRESH)
## ADOO
*Zingiber officinale*
Ginger is a distinctive, knobby root with a hot, sweetish taste. It is an important flavouring in Indian food and should be prepared ahead. The ginger called for in these recipes refers to ginger paste, which is simply the scraped root of green ginger pounded or blended to a paste with preservatives (see below).

Soak the green ginger in hot water for about 30 minutes before scraping it. Never peel ginger, but scrape it as you would a carrot. Fresh ginger is recognised by its juiciness and the ease with which it is scraped. The younger the root, the more delicate its flavour.

**TO STORE fresh ginger** The usual way to store excess root ginger is to plant it in a pot of earth and water daily; it can be removed for use whenever required. Unscraped ginger may be refrigerated in a bag, but I prefer making a ginger paste ready for daily use; this may be frozen for up to 6 months.

**GINGER PASTE** To make enough for 10 dishes, you will need 100 g fresh root ginger, 45 ml (3 tbsp) cooking oil, 60 ml (4 tbsp) water and 30 ml (2 tbsp) salt. Soak the ginger, then scrape and chop into convenient pieces. Place in a food processor or liquidiser and reduce to a smooth paste, adding the oil and water. Lastly, mix in the salt.

**TO STORE paste** Keep in a closed ginger jar for up to 8 weeks in the refrigerator. Ginger paste freezes well for up to 6 months.

# Other important flavourings

## CLARIFIED BUTTER
### GHEE

Ghee is butter in a clarified form suitable for using in vagaars where the butter has to be heated to a high temperature – naturally, ordinary butter would burn. For the same reason, ghee also makes frying less troublesome. Eggs, cutlets, vegetables and Indian sweets are all enhanced by gentle frying in ghee.

Another important advantage is that ghee can be stored at room temperature for over 6 months, a vital factor in India's hot climate.

**TO MAKE GHEE** In a deep saucepan, bring 500 g butter to a gentle boil. Maintain a low to medium temperature and boil the liquid butter for 15 to 20 minutes; it will make a bubbling sound until all the water has evaporated from the ghee. At this stage a layer of scum will rise to the surface, the salt will settle at the bottom and the clarified butter will be in the middle.

Place another container on a flat surface nearby. Remove the ghee from the heat and blow the scum to one side of the saucepan. Pour the clarified butter into the container, leaving the salt at the bottom of the saucepan. The ghee should be crystal clear.

**TO STORE** Cool and store in a steel, enamel or glass container.

**Note** Never leave ghee unattended on the stove-it may boil over and catch alight. Keep children well away.

## COCONUT
### NARIYAL

Coconuts are grown on the tall pinnate-leaved palms (*Cocos nucifera*) found throughout the tropics and believed to have originated in tropical America.

The coconut palm is one of the most important of palms: its leaves provide thatch and straw for weaving hats, baskets, etc; toddy is made from the flowering spathe; coconut oil is used as a hair conditioner; and the fibrous husk of the fruit is made into rope, mats and baskets.

India's palms were originally imported from southeastern Asia and are now cultivated in the coastal regions of the subcontinent.

**IN COOKING** The fresh kernel of the fruit, known as khopra (copra), is used in many dishes. In southern India it is used to flavour fish dishes, as well as the dessert known as halwa. The water of the unripe fruit also makes a refreshing drink.

**OTHER USES** Offerings of fresh coconut called prasad (sanctified food) are distributed in temples
in India, and since it is nutritious food, the flesh of the fresh coconut is recommended for expectant mothers.

**TO OPEN** Choose a husky coconut that is full of milk (you should be able to hear the milk when you shake the coconut). Preheat your oven to 200°C. Puncture three holes in the coconut by hammering a screwdriver through the 'eyes' of the coconut. Drain off the milk (a whitish liquid).

Place the coconut in the heated oven for 15 minutes, then transfer it to a board and use a hammer to split the shell with a hard blow. The shell will fall away from the flesh. Use a knife to lift away any coconut still adhering to the shell.

## SUGAR JAGGERY
### GHOR
A crude raw sugar made from the juice of sugar cane or the sap of certain palm trees. The juice is boiled to obtain purified crystals that are lightly coated with molasses. Golden syrup or ordinary sugar may be substituted for jaggery.

# Fresh herbs in Indian cuisine

## CORIANDER LEAVES
### DHANIA
*Coriandrum sativum*
India's most popular and distinctive herb, coriander leaves, or dhania, is the principal garnish for most dishes. Cooking Indian food without using dhania is like preparing sweets without sugar. An aromatic herb of the parsley family, coriander resembles parsley in appearance, but has a much more pungent flavour. It is available from larger supermarkets. Coriander is also known as Chinese or Japanese parsley. Chop leaves to add to Indian dishes as a garnish.

**To store** Buy coriander in small bunches, remove the roots and store in an airtight container in the refrigerator. Avoid wetting the leaves. Alternatively, place in a damp kitchen towel or damp brown paper and store in the refrigerator for about 1 week.

**To freeze** Wash, clean and chop finely, then place in an ice-cube tray with a little water. Freeze and then store in a plastic bag in the freezer, using the cubes for cooking. Naturally, frozen dhania cannot be used as a garnish.

**To dry** Dry the leaves in the sun until crisp. Grind to a powder and store in an airtight container.

**To clean** Remove the roots and soak in plenty of cold water for about 15 minutes. The soil will settle at the bottom of the dish. Now rinse the herb several times. Chop both stems and leaves finely, and use as required.

**To grow coriander** Buy coriander seeds (specify that you need them for planting), crush lightly and spread over damp, fertile soil. Cover lightly with a layer of soil.

Choose a warm spot, avoiding intense direct sunlight. Coriander may also be grown indoors in pots, but keep the soil damp. The herb should sprout within 14 days. Allow to grow to about 15 cm before harvesting for use or storage.

## FENUGREEK
## METHI BHAJI
*Trigonella foenum-graecum*

Fenugreek, or methi, is a herb with a strong, bitter flavour and aroma. It is sold fresh in small bunches. The leaves are clover shaped, and firmer and darker green than coriander leaves.

**To clean** Use the leaves and only the softer portions of the stem, discarding most of the stem and the roots. Soak in cold water for 15 minutes to allow the soil to settle. Rinse several times before chopping up the herb.

**To store, freeze and grow methi** Use the same method as described for coriander leaves.

**In cooking** The fenugreek herb is particularly valuable for convalescents because of its remedial qualities. It may be used in any dish that requires a bitter taste, or to change the taste of basic recipes such as spiced eggs, potato dishes, puri and poora (spiced pancakes). It also makes a particularly good savoury known as methi moothia.

## MINT
## POODINI (FOODINO)
*Mentha spicata*

The fresh leaves of the commonest garden mint, spearmint or fresh-tasting peppermint are used in much the same manner as in Western cooking. It may also be used as an attractive garnish.

Mint chutneys are popular and the sour milk gravy known as khudi is also improved by the flavour of mint. Fresh mint is an excellent addition to the filling for samoosas and is sometimes used to flavour spiced tea.

Add to young vegetables that are steamed or mix with yoghurt to make a refreshing raita (dip or fresh relish). Also add to fruit punch or soups.

# INDIAN UTENSILS

## BRASS AND COPPER VESSELS

Brass, copper and bell metal saucepans, known as handi, have an essential place in the Indian kitchen. They are either squat or full, wide mouthed or narrow brimmed, and they twinkle and glow as they catch the sunlight.

Handi, the generic term for cooking vessels, is a word used and understood all over India. Handi include certain specific vessels, such as the pateela (a cylindrical pot with a slightly rounded bottom, ranging from a few centimetres to over one metre in diameter) and the parat (a large circular dish with a turned-up rim of 50 to 100 mm). As a rule, Indian cooking vessels are undecorated, because they are scoured with earth and sand before being washed.

Copper pots are often hammered into innumerable little facets that glint like sunlight on a quiet sea. Because of the limited scope for ornamentation, craftsmen have expressed themselves in symmetry of form and fluidity of line. Perfect proportions make each handi a work of art.

Brass is the glory of a Hindu kitchen. Throughout India, however humble the abode, the housewife's kitchen is lit by the glow of her cooking vessels.

Indian cooking utensils are not merely relegated to the kitchen. In the custom of 'Mand', practised in rural Gujerat and Rajasthan, vessels of many types are displayed on shelves in the living room. An Indian girl's dowry always consists of brass and copper utensils, and they are also distributed as gifts on auspicious occasions. In fact, in an Indian household, cooking vessels are as important as china, silver and plate in a Western home.

## Chakki

This is a type of mill consisting of two massive stone discs, one set on the floor and the other above it. It has a wooden handle near the rim and two holes in the centre. The chakki is used specifically for grinding spices and wheat flour but is rare in South Africa today, as food processors have usurped its place.

## Earthenware Vessels

India has an abundance of cheap earthenware. Glazed earthenware in a Persian blue is a speciality in northern India, where centuries ago the Moghuls introduced glazing–a technique of applying ground glass to pottery under heat, making it more durable.

I had the opportunity of staying in a palace in the north where royalty used gold-plated and pure silver utensils, and brass water jugs embedded with precious stones, on a daily basis. But I find India's simple clay pots the most appealing. In a little village in Karnataka, in southern India, I watched with admiration the ease with which one of the potters went about making his matka. First his young helper cleaned and mixed the clay with equal parts of water. He passed a smooth brown clay to the potter, who  squatted on his haunches before his wheel. He cut out a chunk, centred it and with his stick spun the wheel into a blur of motion.

With a flick of his fingers and a curve of his hand, the potter created a perfect, wide-bellied matka before my eyes from a lump of earth in less than a minute. He signed his work and the wheel spun to a halt in a split second. Around him, piles of pots of various shapes and sizes lay drying in the sun. Later they would be dipped briefly into a vat of red dye and stacked for baking in the village kiln.

## Karahai

Similar to a wok, the shape of this large, deep pan facilitates deep frying with only a moderate amount of oil.

## Karchi

A karchi is a long-handled ladle used for lentil cooking and for milk dishes.

## Katori

This earthenware bowl is used for chutneys and soups. Some are made of beaten copper, lined with silver.

## Mortar And Pestle

A wooden, brass or stone set is useful for crushing seeds, making fine chutney or for cracking nuts.

## Rice Spoon

This is a flat, broad spoon of stainless steel shaped like the palm of the hand. Indispensable in the kitchen for braising and stirring, it is the ideal spoon for serving rice.

## Sev Machine

This brass gadget is designed for making Indian savouries such as sev and moorkhoo (deep-fried savoury noodles made from lentil flour). It contains various cutters of different designs.

## Tapela Or Handi

These stackable saucepans, without handles, are made of highly polished brass, copper or aluminium.

## Tawa Or Tavi

This thick iron griddle, either flat or concave, is used for cooking rotis, pancakes and certain savouries. (Rotis may also be made in a heavy-based frying pan.)

## Thali

Stainless steel dining plates are used across India, especially in the villages.

## Vehlan (Rolling Pin)

Light and manageable, the Indian rolling pin is the daintiest in the world. Its pin is 30 cm long, tapered at the ends and widens to 2.5 cm in diameter at the centre.

Indian breads or rotis are rolled out very thinly from small pieces of dough; the vehlan is ideal for this delicate process.

# Indian Savouries

Markets are the essence of life in India—the heartbeat of villages and towns where people gather to shop, chatter and have chaat sessions. Chaat is a term covering the countless salty snacks and hot spicy savouries eaten between meals by Indians everywhere.

In India, every street corner and market is crammed with brightly coloured stalls laden with snacks of infinite variety: spicy batters, deep-fried pastries, puffed rice, roasted nuts and concoctions that have to be tasted to be appreciated. The chaat selection is prodigious.

Visiting an Indian market can be an overwhelming experience. There appear to be as many stalls as there are people. At one end a bangle seller will have a tempting display of cheap yet attractive jewellery, while at the other, a vegetable vendor displays a mound of unusual Indian vegetables.

Between the food stalls you will find piping hot samoosas and spicy pakora frying in oil on iron griddles. Pakora, or chilli bites, are made from sliced aubergines and a variety of vegetables dipped in a mouth-watering lentil-flour batter.

## Chaat Time

For tea lovers, spicy chai stalls are dotted everywhere; friends stop to gossip and drink a C. Cool drink stalls sell brightly coloured cordials, cool thick lassi (a yoghurt drink), mango sherbet, milkshakes and juices. Piles of green coconuts lie heaped by the wayside, ready to be cracked open; their cool juice will quench a dry throat after a satisfying chaat session.

The children of the village are tempted by pyramids of coconut sweets and rows of sweetmeats and other candy-like concoctions. A khulfi wallah—icecream seller—sells his expensive and exotic blends of homemade icecreams, often a mixture of fresh mangoes, walnuts, raisins, almonds and lemons.

Food vendors in India have a most persuasive way of attracting customers: they sing jingles or charming songs, calling passersby to taste their creations. The accompanying music is made by tapping on brass bells and pans. A young vendor of chickpeas, peanuts and lentils will squat in front of his glowing coals, roasting peanuts in their shells. As soon as you show any interest, his face lights up with a smile as he offers chana (roasted chickpeas) in a package of fresh leaves, in exchange for 1 rupee (25 cents).

You meander through, munching the irresistible chana and examining the copper and brass vessels, bright cotton garments and wall hangings, clay pots, beads, incense, silver jewellery and inexpensive leather fantasies. As you walk on, resisting all these tempting goods, beggars bump into you holding out their hands in anticipation, hoping that you will share your chana, your rupees or your compassion.

## Samoosas

Samoosas are, without doubt, the most popular Indian savoury in the Western world. Samoosa-making is an art, demanding paper-thin pur or pastry. The thinnest pastry reaches perfection as it fries into a crispy, many-layered covering for the mouthwatering mince filling.

As there are four stages in samoosa-making (preparing the filling, making the pastry, folding the pastry with filling and frying the samoosa), I suggest that you make the filling a day ahead and keep it refrigerated. For the pastry-making, ask an interested friend to join you. Moral support and an extra pair of hands can be very useful.

**Freezing** Once the samoosas are folded and filled, they may be frozen for up to 6 months. Layer the samoosas between wax paper in a freezable container and seal well. Remove when required and fry directly without thawing.

The filling may also be frozen for a long period. It is suitable for pastry pies and cottage pie as well.

Cut the edge off the samoosa pastry strip

Form a cone and fill with pea filling

Fold over to create a perfect triangle and
ensure that there are no gaps

# SAMOOSA PASTRY | *SAMOOSA PUR*

500 ml (2 cups) cake flour
5 ml (1 tsp) salt
180 ml cold water
60 ml (4 tbsp) cooking oil or ghee
for spreading

Sift the flour and salt. Bind into a firm dough with the cold water.

Divide into eight balls. Place four aside, then roll the remaining four into 150 mm diameter rounds.

Spread each round with 1 t ghee or oil. (Ghee makes a more flavoursome pastry.) Take care to cover each round well, or the pastry will stick together during cooking. Sprinkle lightly with flour. Placing oily sides together, pile one round on top of the other. Once again, spread 1 t oil over the top layer. Sprinkle with flour and place another round (oily side down) on top of the layered rounds. Make a pile of four rounds.

Preheat the oven to 200°C.

Sprinkle a board lightly with flour. Gently roll out the pile of rounds to a 25 cm diameter circle, keeping all the edges together. The pastry may be flipped over during rolling. Place the pile of rounds on an ungreased baking tray and bake in the middle of the oven for 2½ minutes. The pastry will puff up slightly. Remove it from the oven and separate the layers very quickly before they cool. The pastry should be paper thin.

Pile the rounds back on top of each other and cut into strips 60 mm wide. Pile the strips together and cut one short edge to a 45° angle. Wrap the pastry in a damp tea towel to prevent drying, until you are ready to fold the samoosas. Repeat the process with the remaining dough.

**Time: 45 minutes**
**Enough for 32 samoosas**

60 ml (4 tbsp) cake flour
22 ml (1½ tbsp) water

**TO FOLD SAMOOSAS** Make a thick paste with the flour and water. Place the mince filling directly in front of you. Keep a t handy. Practise folding as follows (see illustration and photographs): Place the strip of pastry in front of you on a board with the pointed angle on the lower left-hand side. Bring the line AB to meet line BD. Pinch point C with the other thumb. Keep this pressed and bring line BD down to meet DE. Point C is pressed so there should be no gap in the pocket, otherwise oil will fill into the samoosa while frying, or worse still, the filling will fall out. Holding point E, put 1½ t filling into the samoosa pocket. Continue to fold the samoosa by moving line CE to DF, etc. until all the pastry is folded. Apply a thin layer of flour paste (above) to the edge of the pastry and stick it down onto the samoosa. Repeat with the remaining pastry.

Store in an airtight container in the refrigerator.

**Time for folding: 40 minutes**

**TO FRY SAMOOSAS** Samoosas are usually stored in a freezer. Remove and allow to thaw for about 10 minutes. Pat dry before frying. Using your thumb and forefinger, pinch the samoosa a few times to create a round samoosa pastry. Heat 750 ml cooking oil in a deep saucepan to a moderate temperature. Fry the samoosas slowly until light brown. (To achieve a crispy pastry when frying, it is very important to fry samoosas for at least 7-10 minutes on a medium heat.)

To fry to a crispy coat, use a small saucepan, but deep oil, about a 50 mm drop. After frying to a golden, light colour, allow to cool on a rack, not piling them on top of one another. Place on greaseproof paper or paper towel.

Samoosas are best served hot with a fresh coriander or mint chutney.

**Time for frying: 20 minutes**

# CHICKEN MUSHROOM fILLING

500 g chicken breasts, very finely chopped
150 g mushrooms, chopped
100 g frozen sweetcorn
30 ml (2 tbsp) sago
2 green chillies, finely chopped (add more if preferred)
5 ml (1 tsp) fresh garlic, pounded
8 ml (1½ tsp) fresh ginger, pounded
5 ml (1 tsp) salt
3 ml (½ tsp) turmeric
30 ml (2 tbsp) dhania (coriander) leaves, chopped
60 ml (4 tbsp) ghee or butter
125 ml (½ cup) water

Place all the ingredients in a saucepan, cover and simmer gently for 45 minutes. Leave to cool before using.

Time: 1 hour
Fills 32 samoosas

# MINCE FILLING | *KHIMA FOR SAMOOSAS*

500 g lamb or mutton mince
5 ml (1 tsp) salt
5 ml (1 tsp) fresh ginger, pounded, or
3 ml (½ tsp) fresh garlic, pounded
10 ml (2 tsp) green chillies, pounded
2 medium onions, very finely chopped
30 ml (2 tbsp) ghee or melted butter
1 small bunch dhania (coriander) leaves, washed and finely chopped
30 ml (2 tbsp) green shallot, finely chopped
30 ml (2 tbsp) poodini (mint), finely chopped (optional)
3 ml (½ tsp) gharum masala

Place the mince in a frying pan with salt, ginger or garlic and the green chillies. Cook until the mixture is dry. Add the onions and braise only until all moisture has evaporated.

Add the ghee. The mince should now be fine and dry like breadcrumbs. Leave the mince to cool, then mix in the chopped greens and gharum masala.

**Time: 40 minutes**
**Fills 32 samoosas**

## CHICKEN MINCE FILLING

6 onions (optional)
500 g skinless chicken breast fillets
250 ml (½ cup) water
60 ml (4 tbsp) ghee or sunflower oil
10 ml (2 tsp) green masala
10 ml (2 tsp) fresh garlic, pounded
10 ml (2 tsp) fresh ginger, pounded
10 ml (2 tsp) salt
4 ml (¾ tsp) turmeric
4 carrots, finely chopped in a processor or grated
½ bunch dhania (coriander) leaves, finely chopped
15 ml (3 tsp) lemon juice

If you wish to include onions, chop them into fine pieces, then place in a cloth and squeeze out the juice.

Wash and dry the chicken fillets. In a mincer or food processor, mince finely until smooth. Place in a dish, add water and stir in until the texture is loose and free of lumps.

Heat the ghee in a saucepan. Add ¾ of the quantity of finely chopped onions, then brown gently on a low heat. Add masala, garlic, ginger and salt. Then add the chicken and turmeric. Stir and cook for 20 minutes on a low heat. Do not cover the pot. Allow most of the moisture to evaporate and stir the chicken to ensure a lumpless texture. Then remove from heat.

To give the chicken samoosa a very fresh, crunchy and juicy texture, add the following garnish: the remaining onions, chopped carrots, dhania and lemon juice. Leave to cool. Stir very well.

**Time: 40 minutes**
**Fills 32 samoosas**

A platter of snacks: potato croquettes, samoosas, puri and patra served with lemon wedges and fresh salad greens

# VEGETABLE FILLING

5 ml (3 tbsp) ghee or butter
500 ml (2 cups) frozen peas
2 medium onions, chopped
4 medium potatoes, chopped
4 medium carrots, chopped or grated
5 ml (1 tsp) salt
10 ml (2 tsp) green masala
5 ml (1 tsp) fresh ginger, pounded
8 ml (1½ tsp) fresh garlic, pounded
10 ml (2 tsp) sugar
3 ml (½ tsp) turmeric
15 ml (1 tbsp) tal (sesame seeds)
125 ml (½ cup) dhania (coriander) leaves,
chopped
30 ml (2 tbsp) lemon juice
15 ml (1 tbsp) dhania-jeero (coriander-
cumin)

Heat the ghee in a saucepan. Add the remaining ingredients with half the quantity of coriander leaves. Cover and simmer over a low heat for 45 minutes, stirring occasionally. Allow to cool and mix in the remaining coriander leaves.

**Time: 1 hour**
**Fills 32 samoosas**

# PEA FILLING

1 kg fresh or frozen peas
60 ml (4 tbsp) ghee or butter
5 ml (1 tsp) salt
5 ml (1 tsp) ajowan
10 ml (2 tsp) green masala
5 ml (1 tsp) fresh ginger, pounded
8 ml (1½ tsp) fresh garlic, pounded
15 ml (1 tbsp) sugar
3 ml (½ tsp) turmeric
15 ml (1 tbsp) tal (sesame seeds)
30 ml (2 tbsp) lemon juice
15 ml (1 tbsp) dhania-jeero (coriander-
cumin)
60 ml (4 tbsp) dhania (coriander) leaves,
chopped

Place the frozen peas in a food processor and chop to a course texture.

Heat the ghee in a saucepan. Add the peas. Add the remaining ingredients.

Simmer on a low heat for 45 minutes, stirring occasionally. Allow to cool and mix in the dhania-jeero and coriander leaves.

**Time: 1 hour**
**Fills 32 samoosas**

# FISH FILLING

1 kg fresh firm fish
125 ml (½ cup) cooking oil
2 large onions, sliced
10 ml (2 tsp) green masala
3 ml (½ tsp) turmeric
5 ml (1 tsp) salt
15 ml (1 tbsp) dhania-jeero
(coriander-cumin)
30 ml (2 tbsp) lemon juice
125 ml (½ cup) dhania (coriander)
leaves, chopped

Steam the fish for 5 to 7 minutes. Remove from heat. Remove bones and flake.

Heat the oil in a saucepan, add the onions and fry until soft. Add the fish and remaining ingredients. Cover and gently simmer over a low heat for 15 minutes.

Allow to cool before using.

**Time: 40 minutes**
**Fills 50 samoosas**

# CHILLI BITES | *BHAJIA*

*Bhajia are deep-fried morsels in a spicy lentil-flour batter. Dipped in chilli sauce, they are really special. Experiment with a variety of vegetables. Cubed cheese is a most unusual filling—the spicy melted cheese is a treat. Brinjals and potatoes make the traditional bhajia, but apples and butternut squash are interesting alternatives. Try a bhajia fondue the next time you entertain vegetarians, or non-vegetarians for that matter! The batter and vegetables may be prepared ahead. Serve a variety of fresh chutneys, as well as the refreshing chilli sauce, as sambals.*

### BATTER
375 ml (1½ cups) chana flour
125 ml (½ cup) cake flour, sifted
30 ml (2 tbsp) cooking oil
10 ml (2 tsp) varyari or large soomph (aniseed), crushed
5 ml (1 tsp) baking powder
3 ml (½ tsp) turmeric
10 ml (2 tsp) dhania-jeero (coriander-cumin)
8 ml (1½ tsp) salt
15 ml (1 tbsp) green masala
30 ml (2 tbsp) dhania (coriander) leaves, chopped
200 ml (¾ cup) cold water

### DEEP FRYING
750 ml (3 cups) cooking oil

### VEGETABLES
any vegetable of your choice:
brinjals, with skin
(slice thinly, halve slices and sprinkle with a little salt)
potatoes, peeled (if large, halve, then slice thinly—about 0.5 cm—and sprinkle with salt)
spinach leaves (remove the thick veins and shred)
lettuce, shredded
onions, thinly sliced or cut into rings (looks like calamari when fried)

To make the batter, sift the chana flour into a bowl by the spoonful as it is rather fine and lumpy. Add the cake flour. Heat the oil, then pour it over the flour.

Mix the aniseed, baking powder, turmeric, dhania-jeero, salt, masala and chopped dhania into the flour mixture. Gradually add the water to make a thick batter until it has the consistency of cake mixture. (Add more water if required.)

At this stage the batter may be frozen or kept refrigerated for a few days.

Heat the oil in a pot suitable for deep frying. A good heat is required when frying bhajia.

Dip the vegetables into the batter and coat completely. Gently slide into the heated oil and fry the bhajia until a golden colour on each side. This may take 2 to 3 minutes, depending on the vegetable used and frying about eight at a time (e.g. potatoes take longer to cook than spinach). Remove from oil and drain on paper towel to get rid of excess oil.

Repeat until all the batter has been used. Remember, a good bhajia is light and never doughy!

**Time: 1 hour**
**Makes 35**

Spinach, brinjal, potato, mushroom and lettuce bhajia (chilli bites)

## EASY ONION BHAJIA | *KANDA BHAJIA*

125 ml (½ cup) chana flour
250 ml (1 cup) self-raising flour, sifted
250 ml (1 cup) chopped spinach
2 onions, chopped
2 ml (¼ tsp) turmeric
5 ml (1 tsp) salt
10 ml (2 tsp) dhania-jeero
(coriander-cumin)
10 ml (2 tsp) large soomph (aniseed)
3 ml (½ tsp) red masala
5 ml (1 tsp) green masala
5 ml (1 tsp) ginger, pounded
200 ml (¾ cup) water

Sift the chana flour into a bowl by the spoonful as it tends to be fine and lumpy. Add the self-raising flour. Add the vegetables and spices, then mix well. Gradually stir in the water to make a thick batter, the consistency of cake mixture. (Add more water if required.) At this stage the batter may be frozen or refrigerated for a few days.

Deep fry in the same manner as the Chilli Bites (see previous page). Ensure that the bhajia are fried slowly until they reach a golden colour. Remove from oil and drain on paper towel to get rid of excess oil. Repeat until all the batter has been used.

**Time: 1 hour**
**Makes 35**

## MAIZE FLOUR CHILLI BITES | *VARA*

250 ml (1 cup) maize flour
250 ml (1 cup) chana flour
250 ml (1 cup) semolina or cream of
wheat
15 ml (1 tbsp) sunflower oil
8 ml (1½ tsp) green masala
15 ml (1 tbsp) dhania-jeero
(coriander-cumin)
15 ml (1 tbsp) large soomph (aniseed),
coarsely crushed
3 ml (½ tsp) turmeric
10 ml (2 tsp) salt
125 ml (½ cup) buttermilk
60 ml (4 tbsp) lemon juice
250 ml (1 cup) hot water
60 ml (4 tbsp) chopped dhania
(coriander) leaves
5 ml (1 tsp) bicarbonate of soda or 15 ml
(1 tbsp) fruit salts

Combine the maize flour, chana flour and semolina in a bowl. Mix in the oil, masala and seasonings. Bind with the buttermilk, lemon juice and enough hot water to form a thick batter. Cover the bowl and leave overnight in the refrigerator. The following day, just before frying, mix in the dhania leaves and bicarbonate of soda. Stir well.

Heat the oil in a pot suitable for deep frying. A good heat is required when frying vara. Fry the vara slowly until they are a golden colour. Remove from oil and drain on paper towel to get rid of excess oil.

Repeat until all the batter has been used. Alternatively, the batter may be stored in a refrigerator for up to 4 days.

**Time: 1 hour**
**Makes 48**

# SPINACH BITES | *METHI BHAJEE NA MOOTHIA*

4 bunches (500 g) large-leaved spinach
750 ml (3 cups) chana flour
1 litre (4 cups) maize flour
500 ml (2 cups) white bread flour
45 ml methi (fenugreek) seeds, crushed
in grinder
30 ml (2 tbsp) turmeric
15 ml (1 tbsp) green masala
25 ml (5 tsp) red masala
30 ml (2 tbsp) fresh ginger, pounded
30 ml (2 tbsp) gharum masala
45 ml (3 tbsp) dhania-jeero
(coriander-cumin)
15 ml (1 tbsp) salt
125 ml (½ cup) ghee
250 ml (1 cup) cooking oil for frying

Remove all the stalks then soak the spinach in cold water for a few minutes. Rinse several times or until very clean. (Fresh spinach usually has garden soil stuck to its leaves.)

Chop the spinach leaves quite finely, then place on a large tray and add all the flour and spices with the ghee. Mix well. Add enough water to make a stiff dough. (Be careful not to add too much water, so start with ♦ C and increase gradually.) Using about 1 T of mixture at a time, form thick, finger shapes and keep on a floured tray.

Heat the oil in a saucepan and place as many moothia in the saucepan as possible. Gently fry over a medium heat, turning each moothia over. Remove the fried ones to another pot. When all have been fried, sprinkle ¼C water over the moothia, cover the pot and steam over a very low heat, tossing occasionally for about 15 minutes.

**Time: 1 hour**
**Makes about 24**

# CABBAGE BITES | KHUBI MOOTHIA

½ large head (4 cups) cabbage
500 ml (2 cups) chana flour
250 ml (1 cup) cake flour

625 ml (1½ cups) maize flour

3 ml (½ tsp) bicarbonate of soda
15 ml (1 tbsp) gharum masala
15 ml (1 tbsp) dhania-jeero
(coriander-cumin)
15 ml (1 tbsp) fresh ginger, pounded
10 ml (2 tsp) red masala
5 ml (1 tsp) ground hing (asafoetida)
160 ml (⅓ cup) ghee
250 ml (1 cup) cooking oil for frying

Follow the same method as for Spinach Bites (above).
**Makes about 24**

# SAVOURY VEGETABLE BITES | *METHI BHAJI NA MOOTHIA*

*Chopped methi (obtainable from Indian stores) gives this vegetarian speciality its characteristic bitter flavour. Cabbage may be substituted for the methi for a sweeter moothia.*

300 g (3 bunches) methi (fenugreek)
or 250 g cabbage
125 ml (½ cups) chana flour, sifted
60 ml (4 tbsp) maize meal, sifted
60 ml (4 tbsp) bread flour, sifted
3 ml (½ tsp) baking powder
5 ml (1 tsp) gharum masala
10 ml (2 tsp) dhania-jeero
(coriander-cumin)
3 ml (½ tsp) turmeric
2 ml (¼ tsp) ground hing (asafoetida)
3 ml (½ tsp) fresh ginger, pounded
3 ml (½ tsp) fresh garlic, pounded
5 ml (1 tsp) red masala
5 ml (1 tsp) salt
15 ml (1 tbsp) ghee or butter
250 ml (1 cup) cooking oil for
shallow frying

Remove the roots and thick stems from the methi, then wash and chop finely. If you are using cabbage, wash and chop finely. Place in a bowl.

Mix in the rest of the ingredients until the consistency of a soft dough, then form into cigar shapes, using 2 t of dough at a time.

Heat the oil in a heavy-based pan, then fry the moothia for about 2 to 3 minutes until a crisp coat forms. Put the fried moothia in a small, heavy-based saucepan, cover the pot and cook gently over a very low heat for 15 to 20 minutes, until the moothia are tender.

**Time: 1 hour**
**Serves 4 to 6**

# MAIZE FLOUR NOODLES | *MOORKHOO*

*The tastiest moorkhoo are those my mother used to make for us as children. She perfected a recipe that has been passed on to many people. You need a biscuit machine or icing gun with a star-shaped nozzle.*

750 ml (3 cups) water
15 ml (1 tbsp) butter or margarine
15 ml (1 tbsp) salt
10 ml (2 tsp) ground jeero (cumin)
10 ml (2 tsp) ajowan or jeero (cumin)
seeds
10 ml (2 tsp) tal (sesame seeds)
750 ml (3 cups) ultra-fine maize flour,
sifted (available from Indian stores)
250 ml (1 cup) chana flour, sifted
15 ml (3 tsp) baking powder
750 ml (3 cups) cooking oil for frying

In a small saucepan, combine the water, butter, salt, ground jeero, ajowan and sesame seeds, bring to the boil and set aside.

Mix the dry ingredients in a large bowl, then add the wet mixture. Allow to stand for 30 minutes, then bind into a soft dough.

Heat the oil in a deep saucepan. Fill the machine with the dough and press out onto a board, forming spiral, circular shapes about 75 mm in diameter. (The dough may be pressed out directly into the oil, but the shape will not be as good.) Gently place 6 spirals at a time into the oil.

Fry over a medium heat for about 1½ minutes on each side until the spiral noodles turn golden brown. Remove from the oil and place on paper towel to drain any excess oil. Repeat until all the dough has been used.

Store for up to 3 weeks in an airtight container.

750 ml (3 cups) boiling water
5 ml (1 tsp) butter
10 ml (2 tsp) salt
10 ml (2 tsp) jeero (cumin) seeds
5 ml (1 tsp) tal (sesame seeds)
900 ml ultra-fine maize flour, sifted
(available from Indian stores)
125 ml (½ cup) chana flour, sifted
750 ml (3 cups) sunflower oil for frying

VARIATION
Follow the method for Moorkhoo above.

# SPICY TAMARIND-WATER PURI | *PANI PURI*

*Pani means water. A pani puri is a little round, fried, puffed bread filled with tart, spicy tamarind water—an exciting way to quench your thirst under the hot summer sun! Pop the whole pani puri into your mouth and experience a delightfully cool sensation down your throat. It makes a lovely starter or snack.*

### SPICY TAMARIND SAUCE
100 g tamarind pulp
750 ml (3 cups) water
15 ml (1 tbsp) sugar
15 ml (1 tbsp) jeero (cumin seeds), finely crushed
10 ml (2 tsp) chilli powder

### DOUGH
a double quantity standard Puri recipe (page 59), i.e. 500 ml (2 cups) flour
cooking oil for deep frying

For the sauce, soak the tamarind pulp in 1 cup water for 10 minutes. Strain the thick pulp into a container and discard the pips. Add 2 cups water and stir.

Add the sugar, jeero and chilli powder. Mix well and place in the refrigerator to cool.

Divide the puri dough into 30 parts and roll them into very small rounds, 50 mm in diameter. Deep fry in hot oil; the puri should puff up.

Pierce a hole in each puri ball and fill it with the spicy sauce.

**Time: 1 hour**
**Makes 30**

# POTATO CROQUETTES | *BATAKA TIKKIE*

*These little cumin-flavoured potato croquettes are served hot with chutney or tomato sauce.*

8 medium potatoes
3 slices stale white bread, soaked in 250 ml (1 cup) cold water
8 ml (1½ tsp) green masala or 3 green chillies, finely chopped
10 ml (2 tsp) salt
10 ml (2 tsp) jeero (cumin seeds), coarsely crushed
125 ml (½ cup) dhania (coriander) leaves, chopped, or 125 ml (½ cup) mint, chopped
cooking oil for shallow frying

Boil the potatoes in as little water as possible until cooked. Peel and mash until smooth.

Squeeze the water from the soaked bread, then add it to the mashed potato. Mix well with the seasoning to form a firm mixture. Roll about 1 T of the mash mixture into a round, then press flat. Repeat until all the mixture has been used.

Heat a 12-mm layer of oil in a pan. Fry four potato croquettes at a time until brown on both sides. Reheat the oil and fry the rest. Always ensure that the oil remains hot, or the mash may disintegrate. It also releases moisture, so do not fry more than four at a time.

**Time: 40 minutes**
**Makes 16 to 18**

# SPICED PURI | *TIKHEE PURI*

*Spiced biscuits are ideal to serve at teatime or as snacks.*

500 ml (2 cups) cake flour, sifted
125 ml (½ cup) semolina or
cream of wheat
3 ml (½ tsp) turmeric
5 ml (1 tsp) green masala or green
chillies, finely chopped
8 ml (1½ tsp) salt
5 ml (1 tsp) jeero (cumin seeds), crushed
80 ml (⅓ cup) ghee or melted
margarine
180 ml warm water
cooking oil for deep frying

Mix all the ingredients well, rubbing in ghee with your fingertips until it has the texture of crumbs. Use sufficient warm water to make a soft pliable dough, then knead well.

Form small, walnut-sized balls and roll them out into 5 mm thick rounds, 75 mm in diameter. Using a knife, make a few 1 cm cuts in the centre of the puri (the cuts prevent it from puffing up during frying). Deep fry on both sides in heated oil, until light brown.

Store in an airtight container for up to 2 weeks.

**Time: 1 hour**
**Makes 25**

500 ml (2 cups) cake flour, sifted
5 ml (1 tsp) green chillies, chopped
10 ml (2 tsp) jeero (cumin seeds),
crushed
10 ml (2 tsp) tal (sesame seeds)
10 ml (2 tsp) salt
175 ml ice-cold water to bind

VARIATION — JEERA PURI
Remember to use cold instead of warm water. Follow the method for Spiced Puri. Alternatively, roll out the dough to a 3 mm thickness, cut into squares and fry.

# STEAMED SEMOLINA SAVOURY | *KHAMAN DOKRI*

*You will need a steamer in order to prepare these sponge-textured, savoury cubes.*

625 ml (2½ cup) semolina or cream
of wheat
30 ml (2 tbsp) cooking oil
5 ml (1 tsp) green masala
5 ml (1 tsp) fresh ginger, pounded
10 ml (2 tsp) sugar
3 ml (½ tsp) turmeric
2 ml (¼ tsp) ground hing (asafoetida)
250 ml (1 cup) corn kernels
a pinch salt
500 ml (2 cups) buttermilk
15 ml (1 tbsp) fruit salts

VAGAAR
125 ml (½ cup) cooking oil
10 ml (2 tsp) tal (sesame seeds)
5 ml (1 tsp) rai (mustard seeds)

GARNISH
45 ml (3 tbsp) desiccated coconut
45 ml (3 tbsp) dhania (coriander) leaves,
chopped

In a large bowl, combine the semolina or cream of wheat, oil, masala, ginger, sugar, turmeric, asafoetida, corn kernels and salt. Pour in the buttermilk, mix well and allow to stand for 1 hour.

Add the fruit salts and mix well.

Grease two layers of a steam cooker and pour the khaman mixture into both pans. Pour water into the steamer, put the pans on top, cover and cook over a medium heat for 20 minutes. The mixture should have a firm, spongy texture. Remove from the heat, cut both layers into smallish cubes, then arrange on a platter.

For the vagaar, heat the oil in a small saucepan, then add the sesame and mustard seeds. Pour the oil over the cubed khaman and garnish with coconut and dhania leaves.

Alternatively, sprinkle fine sev (savoury noodles) and lemon juice over the dish and serve it with fine onion rings.

**Time: 1½ hours, plus 1 hour standing**
**Serves 4 to 6**

Light and fluffy steamed semolina savoury

# FRIED PEANUTS | *FRIED SHINGH*

500 g raw peanuts with red skins
cooking oil for deep frying
3 ml (½ tsp) red chilli powder
5 ml (1 tsp) salt

Deep fry the peanuts for 1 to 2 minutes. Remove, drain on absorbent paper and season with chilli powder and salt.

**Time: 20 minutes**
**Makes 500 g**

# SPICY GRILLED PEANUTS | *SPICY SHINGH*

500 g raw peanuts with red skins
10 ml (2 tsp) salt
3 ml (½ tsp) red chilli powder

Wash the peanuts in cold water. Drain in a colander. Rub in salt and spread them on a tray. Leave to dry in the sun for 4 to 8 hours.

Preheat the oven to 140°C. Sprinkle the peanuts on an oven tray on the middle shelf of the oven. Leave to dry completely (25 minutes), then remove and season with chilli powder.

Store in an airtight container.

**Time: 30 minutes, plus 4 to 8 hours drying**
**Makes 500 g**

# CHICKEN PIECES IN BATTER | *MURGHI NA PAKORA*

*I serve these chicken pieces dipped and fried in a spicy lentil batter as a hot starter or cocktail snack, with a tangy chilli sauce for dipping.*

500 g chicken, cubed into 12-mm pieces
5 ml (1 tsp) salt
5 ml (1 tsp) fresh ginger, pounded
5 ml (1 tsp) fresh garlic, pounded
8 ml (1½ tsp) green masala
5 ml (1 tsp) dhania-jeero (coriander-cumin)
3 ml (½ tsp) turmeric
5 ml (1 tsp) lemon juice
750 ml (3 cups) cooking oil for deep frying

BATTER

750 ml (3 cups) self-raising flour, sifted
3 ml (½ tsp) salt
2 ml (¼ tsp) turmeric
30 ml (2 tbsp) dhania (coriander)
leaves, chopped
200 ml (¾ cup) cold water

Wash and drain the chicken pieces. Mix with the seasonings and set aside.

For the batter, mix the flour with the salt, turmeric and coriander leaves, then bind with the water until the thick batter has a flowing consistency.

Heat the oil in a deep saucepan. Test by placing a drop of batter into the oil: if it shoots up to the surface immediately, the oil is ready. Dip each piece of chicken into the batter. Coat well and gently place into the oil. Fry for 2 minutes or until a crisp, brown jacket has formed. Remove and drain on absorbent paper.

**Time: 45 minutes**
**Serves 4**

# FISH CAKES | *MACHI TIKKA*

*Serve these fish cakes as a hot snack with chutney or tomato sauce and thick wedges of lemon.*

1 kg filleted hake
2 slices stale white bread, soaked in
250 ml (1 cup) water
1 large onion, finely chopped
125 ml (½ cup) dhania (coriander)
leaves, chopped
60 ml (¼ cup) shallots, finely
chopped (optional)
13 ml (2½ tsp) green masala
5 ml (1 tsp) turmeric
8 ml (1½ tsp) fresh garlic, pounded
10 ml (2 tsp) lemon juice
10 ml (2 tsp) salt
2 eggs, beaten
250 ml (1 cup) cooking oil for frying

Cover the fish with boiling water and allow to stand for 10 minutes. Strain and flake the fish, removing all bones.

Squeeze all the moisture from the soaked bread, then crumble. Squeeze out excess moisture from the onion. Add the bread, onion, dhania, shallots, masala, turmeric, garlic, lemon juice and salt to the fish and mix well. Fold the eggs into the mixture. At this stage, the mixture may be frozen until needed.

With the palm of your hand, roll the fish mixture into small balls, about the size of a walnut. Press flat and shallow fry over medium heat until golden brown on both sides.

# INDIAN BREADS

Roti-making—a ritual usually performed just before or even during dinner—is a special part of every Indian cook's day. If she is in a good mood, her family will be privileged to be seated at the table while she lifts piping hot rotis off the tavi (griddle) with a flick of her iron-tipped fingers. Love fuels the perfectionism demanded if her rotis are to be light and airy masterpieces. Her concentration may even be called 'sacred', as she rolls out the thin discs of dough with expert motions of her rolling pin.

This dainty rolling pin is a far cry from the robust model of her Western counterpart, but can still prove most effective, as my brothers will bear out. Years ago my eldest brother managed to incur my gentle mother's wrath as she prepared roti. My sister and I took shelter as the pin flew across the room at my brother. He dived clear, but at that moment my elder sisters arrived home to meet the flying missile as unsuspecting targets. The tip of my eldest sister's beautiful nose bears testimony to this family memory!

Indian breads—roti, chapati, foolka, puri and naan—are extremely important in an Indian meal and may even be regarded as a course on their own, so large a part do they play, particularly in northern India.

## USING YEAST

Like all plants, yeast has a life of its own and should be treated with respect. It reacts unfavourably to certain conditions, including high temperatures, salt, moisture and the extra fat or sugar of richer doughs. Optimum growth is ensured by adhering to a few basic rules.

Always use tepid water to dissolve the yeast. Hot water kills yeast instantly, while too low a temperature will discourage it from growing.

The cook provides food for the yeast in the form of flour. As the yeast grows, it produces expanding air bubbles which are the ideal raising agent for the dough.

Keep the dough in a warm place – an airing Cboard or a warming drawer, or even an airtight plastic container. (My mother always wrapped the container in a small blanket, an old-fashioned method that still works well.)

Because salt kills yeast, avoid direct contact between the two. Always combine the salt well with the flour before adding the yeast mixture.

Moisture also affects yeast growth. Flours of varying quality absorb different amounts of liquid. Always use sufficient tepid liquid to form a soft, but not tight, elastic texture. Remember that soft dough rises quickly, while a tight dough makes for very heavy bread.

## ROTI DOUGH

*This roti dough is made using a food processor or food mixer.*

500 ml (2 cups) cake flour, sifted
3 ml (½ tsp) salt
60 ml (4 tbsp) cooking oil
160-250 ml (²/₃–1 cup) hot water

Place the flour and salt in a food processor. Aerate by running the machine for a few seconds. Add oil, then pulse again. Gradually add the water to bind the dough, which should have a firm texture.

Follow the method for Roti (page 57) for making this bread.
**Makes 10**

## HEALTH ROTI

500 ml (2 cups) brown flour, sifted
3 ml (½ tsp) salt
160-250 ml (²/₃–1 cup) hot water

Place the flour and salt in a food processor. Aerate by running the machine for a few seconds. Gradually add the water to bind the dough, which should have a firm texture. Dip your fingertips in oil to help you smooth down the sticky dough. This dough tends to be tacky since it has no oil or ghee added.

Follow the method for Roti (page 59) for making the breads.
**Makes 10**

 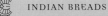

# RICH FLAKY UNLEAVENED BREAD | *PARATHA*

*If you are concerned about cholesterol, perhaps you should stay away from this flaky, butter-enriched bread! In India it is baked in a tandoori oven and is the ideal accompaniment to such classic meat dishes as mutton tarkhari or kebaabs.*

375 ml (1½ cups) cake flour, sifted
5 ml (1 tsp) salt
90 ml (6 tbsp) melted ghee
approx 125 ml (½ cup) hot water
60 ml (4 tbsp) ghee for spreading

Place the flour in a bowl. Work in the salt and melted ghee with your fingertips. Mix in enough water to form a soft dough. Knead for a few minutes, then divide the dough into two portions and shape into balls.

Roll one portion into a large round on a lightly floured board, then roll to the size of a dinner plate. Spread with 1 T ghee, lightly sprinkle with flour and make fingertip imprints on the dough. Roll into a sausage shape, then roll each end in the opposite direction, forming an 'S' shape. Place one rolled up end onto the other and press on a lightly floured board. Roll this mound to the size of a dinner plate. Repeat with the second portion of dough.

Heat a tavi or heavy frying pan. Cook the paratha on an ungreased tavi or pan until freckled with golden spots on both sides. Spread ½ T ghee on either side and cook for a further 10 seconds on both sides.

Remove from the tavi, then squash the paratha gently between your hands to make it flake. Serve warm with meat dishes. Reheat by warming on a heated tavi or pan for 1½ minutes on each side.

### VARIATION
To make a triangular-shaped paratha, roll one portion of dough into a large round the size of a dinner plate. Spread with 1 T melted ghee, sprinkle with flour and make fingertip imprints.

Fold the round paratha in half. Spread 2 t melted ghee over this half, sprinkle with flour, then fold in half again, forming a triangle. Roll this into a large triangle and cook as above.
**Time: 30 minutes**

# UNLEAVENED BREAD | *ROTI*

*Roti, also known as chapati, is a flat, unleavened Indian bread, which is prepared almost daily in an Indian home. To eat roti, break off a piece and wrap it around a little curry or tarkhari. Rotis are served with most Indian dishes.*

125 ml (½ cup) white bread flour, sifted and 125 ml (½ cup unsifted brown flour or 250 ml (1 cup) bread flour only
3 ml (½ tsp) salt
60 ml (4 tbsp) melted ghee or margarine
80 ml (⅓ cup) hot water
80 ml (⅓ cup) ghee for spreading

Sift the flour and salt into a bowl. Pour the melted ghee into the flour and rub to a breadcrumb texture. Add the water to bind the flour into a soft, pliable dough. Knead briefly on a lightly floured board.

Divide the dough into 3 balls. Roll out each to a 75 mm round. Spread with 1 t ghee. Punch the round with your fingers to form dents. Sprinkle lightly with flour. Form an air pocket by lifting and gathering the edges of the round together, then press flat. Roll evenly into a 175 mm diameter round. Repeat with the other two rounds of dough.

Heat a tavi or roti griddle. (Use a large pan if a tavi is not available.) Place one roti on the ungreased tavi and cook for about 4 to 5 minutes, turning the roti over until it loses its 'wet' look. The roti should puff up, forming two layers; press it with a spatula to encourage the puffing.

Remove from the griddle and spread with 1½ t ghee on either side. Repeat for the other rotis.

Rotis may be served warm or cold. To reheat, place a roti on a hot griddle for a few moments.
**Time: 30 minutes**
**Makes 3**

Triangular-shaped naan grilled in the oven

# OVEN-BAKED BREAD | *NAAN*

*This rich, round bread, topped with sesame seeds, is traditionally baked in a tandoori oven.*
*Hot naan is delicious with meat and chicken tarkhari. I like to spread garlic or savoury butter on*
*naan.*

1 kg (4 cups) cake flour, sifted
5 ml (1 tsp) salt
1 packet instant dried yeast
15 ml (1 tbsp) jeero (cumin seeds)
60 ml (4 tbsp) melted ghee
125 ml (½ cup) sugar
3 eggs
500 ml (2 cups) milk
15 ml (1 tbsp) tal (sesame seeds)

Mix the flour and salt in a large bowl. Add the yeast and jeero, then mix well. In a smaller bowl, whip the ghee, sugar and 2 eggs together until light and fluffy, or mix in a food processor.

Add the egg mixture to the flour and yeast, then mix into a soft, sticky dough with the milk. Be careful: if the dough is too soft it will spread and not rise. Leave the dough for approximately 1½ to 2 hours in a warm, draught-free area to double its size.

When the dough has risen, punch it down and knead. Divide into six rounds, place on a large, greased tray and leave for approximately1 hour to rise again. Beat the remaining egg and gently brush over the rounds of dough. Sprinkle with sesame seeds. Bake in a preheated oven at 180°C, on the middle shelf, for 15 minutes.
**Time: 30 minutes, plus up to 2 hours rising**

# PUFFED FRIED BREAD | *PURI*

50 ml (1 cup) cake flour, sifted
3 ml (½ teaspoon) salt
80 ml (⅓ cup) ghee or melted butter
30 ml (2 tablespoons) warm milk
45 ml (3 tablespoons) hot water
750 ml (3 cups) cooking oil for deep frying

Mix the flour and salt, and work in the ghee with your fingertips. Bind into a soft dough with the milk and water.

Divide the dough into 10 balls. Roll each one out evenly on a lightly floured board to a diameter of 75 mm.

Heat the oil in a karahai or deep saucepan. Fry four puri at a time, using a slotted ladle to press them under the oil; this helps them to puff up. Fry the puri for 1 minute on each side. Remove and drain on absorbent paper.

Puri are delicious when eaten hot, but they may also be served cool.

**Time: 30 minutes**
**Serves 2 to 3**

# RICH SWEET ROTI | *MITTHI ROTI*

*This small lentil-filled roti, flavoured with crushed aniseed and butter,
is usually eaten as a first course in a vegetarian meal.*

### LENTIL FILLING
250 ml (1 cup) oil lentils
5 ml (1 tsp) large soomph (aniseed),
coarsely crushed
5 ml (1 tsp) elachi (cardamom)
seeds, crushed
3 ml (½ tsp) white pepper
200 ml (¾ cup) sugar

### DOUGH
500 ml (2 cups) cake flour, sifted
5 ml (1 tsp) salt
120 ml (8 tbsp) melted ghee
160 ml (²/₃ cup) hot water
125 ml (½ cup) melted ghee for
spreading over roti and as a dip

Pick over the lentils and soak in 2 cups boiling water for
30 minutes. Wash several times, removing loose husks. Boil the
lentils in 1½ cups water for 20 minutes in a covered saucepan
(1 t oil in the water will stop it from boiling over). The lentils will
reduce to a thick mass.

Add the soomph, cardamom, pepper and sugar. Stir and
simmer for 20 minutes, allowing excess moisture to evaporate.
The lentil filling should be thick and fairly dry. Remove from
the heat and leave to cool before use.

To make the roti dough, place the flour in a bowl, add salt
and ghee, then rub to a fine texture. Bind into a soft dough
with the water, knead well and divide into 8 balls. Flatten and
roll each ball to a 10 cm diameter, on a lightly floured board.

Place 2 tbsp lentil filling in the centre of each round. Lift the
edges and gather, pinching together to form a pocket. Press
gently and roll lightly to a 20 cm diameter roti. Set aside.
Repeat with the rest of the dough and lentil filling.

Heat a tavi or large frying pan to a moderate heat. Gently
place a roti on the ungreased tavi and cook for 1 to 2 minutes
on either side until the roti's 'wet' look has given way to a
golden, freckled appearance.
Spread with 1 tsp ghee on either side. Cook the remaining roti
and keep warm in a warming drawer until needed.

Place ½ cup melted ghee on the dinner table as a dip for the
roti.

**Time: 1 to 1½ hours**
**Serves 6**

# SPICY POTATO ROTI | *ALU ROTI*

*In India, alu roti would be alu naan as it is usually cooked in a tandoori oven. This chilli-flavoured roti is a pleasant change from the plain roti eaten daily.*

2 x quantity Roti Dough (page 57)
melted ghee or butter for spreading

FILLING
60 ml (4 tbsp) cooking oil
3 ml (½ tsp) rai (mustard seeds)
10 limri (curry leaves)
2 onions, chopped
6 large potatoes, peeled and cubed
5 ml (1 tsp) salt
5 ml (1 tsp) green masala
375 ml (1½ cups) warm water

Heat the oil in a saucepan. Quickly add the rai and limri. After a few seconds, add the onions. Stir and cook for 2 minutes.

Add the potatoes, salt and masala, then add the water and allow to simmer for 20 minutes until all moisture has evaporated. Stir again and mash the potato mixture until smooth. Remove from the heat.

Prepare the roti dough, then divide into 6 portions. Roll each portion out to a 100 mm diameter. Place 1 heaped T potato filling in the centre of each. Gather the edges of each roti, lift and press together to form a pocket. Press gently.

Roll each roti gently on a lightly floured board into a round the size of a side plate or about 150 mm in diameter.

Heat a tavi griddle or frying pan to a temperature that is still comfortable when your hand is placed over it for a few seconds. Carefully place a roti on the pan. Cook for 2 minutes until a few bubbles appear. Rotate the roti and cook for another minute. Flip the roti over gently using a spatula, ensuring that the roti does not break. Cook for another 2 minutes.

Spread melted ghee or butter on the top and serve warm.

**Time: 1½ hours**
**Serves 6**

# FRIED YEAST BREAD | FOOLKA

*For these puffed rounds of fried bread, flavoured with cumin, the yeast dough must be prepared 1 to 2 hours ahead. Foolka and kebaabs (mince balls) complement each other perfectly, though foolka may be served with any other dish.*

60 ml (4 tbsp) cooking oil
15 ml (3 tsp) jeero (cumin seeds)
5 ml (1 tsp) salt
15 ml (1 tbsp) sugar
1 kg (4 cups) cake flour, sifted
1 packet instant dried yeast
500 to 750 ml (2 to 3 cups) lukewarm water
750 ml (3 cups) cooking oil for frying

Rub the oil, jeero, salt and sugar into the flour with your fingertips. Add the yeast, then bind into a soft dough with the water. Place a little oil on your fingertips, especially if the dough feels tacky.

Place the dough in an airtight container and leave to rise for 1½ hours.

When the dough has risen, sprinkle the rolling surface generously with flour. Roll a small handful of dough as evenly as possible to a 5 mm thickness and cut into rounds approximately 50 mm in diameter, using a biscuit cutter, or the mouth of a wide glass tumbler. Place the rounds onto a floured tray until you have your required quantity of foolka. Do not place them on top of each other in case they stick together. Any remaining dough may be stored in a plastic bag or container and frozen until required.

Heat sufficient oil for deep frying in a karhai or pot. Use a smaller pot for frying so that the oil will be deep enough. Gently drop each foolka into the oil, fry for a few seconds and tap with a slotted spoon until it puffs up. Flip over and fry for a few seconds until light brown. The foolka should puff up completely in the oil. Remove and drain on absorbent paper.

**Time: 1 hour, plus overnight rising**
**Serves 8**

TIPS
Cover foolka to prevent them from becoming hard. Serve them with marmalade, or for a savoury snack, top them with cheese.

# Easy Health Breads

Bread-making is not difficult if you understand the fundamentals. Even beginners can accomplish the simple techniques.

When using yeast in any recipe, do not to use hot water to bind the dough. Lukewarm water, sugar and heat allow the yeast to grow rapidly, thus creating a well-rounded loaf. Bread can be made within 2 hours if you leave the raw dough to rise in a warm place. Heat the oven for 5 minutes on 200 °C, then switch off. Put the bread in this oven to rise. Alternatively, find the sunniest spot in your home, even in the direct sun, and cover with a fine muslin cloth. The dough should rise well in about 45 minutes. A useful tip is to grease a loaf pan, line it with greaseproof paper and dust with flour before putting the raw dough in for rising.

Try the following recipes with any flour of your choice: for a health loaf use nutty wheat flour, for a seed loaf use brown bread flour, and for a farmhouse loaf try cake flour. Ingredients to keep handy are sunflower seeds, sesame seeds, poppy seeds, flax seeds, raisins, nuts and honey.

I always use a food mixer to sift the flour by running the machine with a dough hook. Thereafter I bind the dough as it incorporates air, making the bread lighter. More importantly, I use much less of my energy as there is no necessity to knead the dough by hand.

You don't need to bake the full amount of dough once you have made it. Place half the amount in a bag and freeze it. When needed again, leave to thaw at room temperature. Place in a loaf pan to rise, then bake.

To cut the bread evenly, turn the loaf onto its rounded side and cut along the even underside.

# FARMHOUSE LOAf

1 kg (4 cups) cake flour
10 ml (2 tsp) salt
10 ml (2 tsp) sugar
1 packet instant dried yeast
15 ml (3 tsp) jeero (cumin seeds)
(optional)
45 ml (3 tbsp) cooking oil
330 ml (1⅓ cups) lukewarm (not hot)
water

Sift the flour, salt and sugar in a food mixer (otherwise bind by hand), then mix in the yeast and jeero seeds. Add the oil and mix well. Slowly add just enough water to bind into a soft, sticky, dropping mixture (not a stiff dough). Transfer to a greased baking dish and leave to rise for 1 hour or until it doubles in size. Bake in a preheated oven at 180°C for 45 to 60 minutes and brown on top. If you tap the bread it should sound hollow. Remove from the oven and cover with a clean cloth to keep the bread soft. Leave to cool before slicing.
**Makes 1 large loaf**

# BROWN HEALTH BREAD

ingredients as per Farmhouse Loaf
(above) but use nutty wheat or brown
flour instead of cake flour
15 ml (1 tbsp) sunflower seeds
10 ml (2 tsp) sesame seeds
10 ml (2 tsp) flax seeds
a handful raisins (optional)
poppy seeds for sprinkling

Mix together the flour, sunflower, sesame and flax seeds, and raisins (if using). Follow the recipe for Farmhouse Loaf (above). Before you leave the bread to rise, sprinkle over a handful of poppy, sunflower and sesame seeds. Press them down onto the raw dough so that they do not fall off after the bread is baked.
**Makes 2 small loaves**

# RICH FARMHOUSE LOAf

ingredients as per Farmhouse Loaf (top)
2 eggs, beaten
lukewarm milk for binding

Follow the recipe for Farmhouse Loaf (top), add the eggs to the mixture after sifting. Bind with milk. Once the dough is in the baking dish, brush a little egg over the top and leave to rise.

# FRESH, OVEN-BAKED SCONES

500 ml (2 cups) self-raising flour, sifted
3 ml (½ tsp) salt
15 ml (3 tsp) sugar
10 ml (2 tsp) baking powder
10 ml (2 tsp) soft butter or margarine
15 ml (1 tbsp) sunflower oil
2 eggs, whisked
milk for binding

Mix together the flour, salt, sugar and baking powder. Add the butter and oil, then mix. Stir in the eggs and milk, to form a very soft dough. To ensure light scones, use quick hand movements when binding the dough. 'Pressing' the dough will result in a tough texture.

Spoon about 1 tbsp (heaped) dough into a muffin pan, or greased baking tray. Brush each with egg and bake at 200°C in a preheated oven for about 15 minutes.
**Makes 12 medium scones or 1 large loaf**

# Soups

Soups are probably the easiest dishes to make, especially if you use a pressure cooker. Bony meat and chicken soups make excellent meals in a pressure cooker and it reduces cooking time.

Start by making a vagaar in the pressure cooker and after braising the marinated lamb, add just about everything else. Cook on high pressure for about 30 to 40 minutes and you will have a nutritious soup that can be served over rice.

Organically grown vegetables are first choice. I have yet to taste anything like the spinach I grow in my own vegetable garden.

The secret to good, wholesome soups is to use the correct blend of spices and to garnish with the freshest herbs available. For extra nutrient value, chop up celery, parsley and fresh herbs—straight from the garden if possible. Use fresh mint for meat soups, coriander for chicken soup and fenugreek with vegetable soup.

Are soups comparable to the Indian dhals? Dhal is the most important lentil gravy accompaniment to steaming hot rice in India, with a unique texture, and should not be mistaken for soup, which is eaten as a main meal.

# BAKED GARLIC CROUTONS

90 ml (6 tbsp) butter or margarine
8 ml (1½ tsp) fresh garlic, pounded
½ loaf white bread, sliced

Preheat the oven to 180°C.

Mix together the butter and garlic, then spread over the bread slices. Cut the slices into cubes and arrange on a baking tray. Bake in the centre of the oven for 15 minutes until golden brown and crisp. Remove and leave to cool. Store in an airtight container.

**Time: 25 minutes**
**Serves 6**

# CHICKEN SOUP | *MURGHI SOUP*

*This makes a filling meal when served with small bowls of steaming rice.*

1.5 kg chicken
45 ml (3 tbsp) ghee or melted margarine
6 elachi (cardamom pods)
2 onions, chopped
3 ml (½ tsp) turmeric
10 ml (2 tsp) salt
10 ml (2 tsp) black pepper
10 ml (2 tsp) fresh ginger, pounded
1.5 litres (6 cups) hot water
250 ml (1 cup) cubed pumpkin
2 tomatoes, grated
45 ml (3 tbsp) dhania (coriander) leaves, chopped
15 ml (1 tbsp) parsley, chopped

Wash and cut up the chicken into small, bite-size pieces.

Heat the ghee in a large, deep saucepan. Fry the elachi for a few seconds, then add the onions and brown for 2 minutes.

Add the chicken, turmeric, salt, pepper and ginger. Toss for 3 minutes. Add the water, pumpkin, tomatoes, dhania and parsley. Simmer for 1 hour until the vegetables and chicken are cooked.

Add extra water if necessary.

**Time: 1½ hours**
**Serves 6**

# VEGETABLE SOUP | *BHAJI SOUP*

*An easy, nourishing soup to prepare for a cold winter's night, serve it with croutons or toast.*

125 ml (½ cups) pearl barley
2 onions, chopped
125 ml (½ cup) melted ghee or margarine
1 tomato, chopped
500 ml (2 cups) mixed vegetables, diced
1 green chilli, finely chopped
2 ml (¼ tsp) white pepper
5 ml (1 tsp) fresh ginger, pounded
5 ml (1 tsp) fresh garlic, pounded
3 ml (½ tsp) turmeric
5 ml (1 tsp) salt
1 litre (4 cups) water
30 ml (2 tbsp) parsley, chopped

GARNISH
30 ml (2 tbsp) dhania (coriander) leaves, chopped

Soak the barley in some warm water for about 30 minutes, then drain.

Fry the onions gently in ghee until brown. Add the barley and the remaining ingredients. Simmer for 1 hour on a medium heat. If a smooth soup is preferred, liquidise.

Garnish with dhania before serving.

**Time: 1 hour**
**Serves 4**

# NECK OF LAMB SOUP | *GOSHT SOUP*

*This is a nourishing and heartening soup, ideal for children or convalescents. Garnish with croutons.*

500 g neck of lamb
2 litres (8 cups) water
5 ml (1 tsp) fresh garlic, pounded
10 ml (2 tsp) fresh ginger, pounded
8 ml (1½ tsp) salt
10 ml (2 tsp) pepper
3 ml (½ tsp) turmeric
1 onion, chopped
3 tomatoes, chopped
125 ml (½ cup) pearl barley
2 stalks celery, chopped
1 turnip, chopped
30 ml (2 tbsp) parsley or mint, chopped

Wash the meat and cut it into small pieces.

Bring the water to the boil, add all the ingredients and simmer for 2 hours until the meat is tender. Add more water if the soup thickens.

**Time: 2 hours**
**Serves 6**

# Poultry & Meat

The buying and handling of meat  is part of the fundamental training for a young Indian girl; it is particularly important that the meat be washed well in several rinses of water. In some instances my mother would even rub a little salt over the meat to remove dried blood and other impurities.

Meat, like fish, is preferably cooked on the bone to preserve flavour.

Although many Indian recipes call for a chicken that is cut into pieces, it is better to buy a whole chicken and cut it up yourself. Whole chickens are more flavoursome because they have lost none of their juices. Choose a full-breasted bird in a dry pack.

Indian recipes call for a chicken to be cut evenly into 16 pieces or 30 smaller, bite-sized ones. I was taught the Indian method at an early age, and it is not as difficult a task as it sounds. With practice, you should be able to cut up a chicken in 3 to 5 minutes. Chicken pieces are important in Indian cooking, allowing the spices to penetrate the flesh and avoiding a bland, boiled taste. The bone is important, as it adds to the flavour of the gravy.

Remove the giblet pack from inside the cavity. Wash the bird under running water and pat dry with absorbent paper. Place a cutting board on a work surface, with a cloth spread underneath to prevent slipping. Place the chicken on the board with breast uppermost and legs facing you. Trim off excess skin from the neck and any fat from the cavity.

Feel the chicken to locate a thigh joint. Hold the leg firmly in one hand and cut through the skin between the leg and breast with a sharp knife. Pull the thigh bone out and press hard, upwards, to pop the joint. Cut through the ball and socket thigh joint, removing the thigh and leg from the body. Cut through the knee joint, thus dividing each leg portion into two – drumstick and thigh.

To cut off a wing, stand the bird upright with the breast still facing you. Hold the wing in one hand and locate the shoulder joint near the side of the neck. Look for a slight indentation, prod with the knife until it slips into the joint. Cut through, taking a long piece of flesh from the side of the bird. Divide the wing joints into two by cutting through the second joint from the wingtip. Then cut off the fillet of the chicken. Repeat with the other wing, this time standing the chicken upright with the backbone facing you. Remove the wingtips and discard.

Place the bird with the back facing you, then feel for the protruding backbone. Slip the knife under it and cut towards the neck on either side, to loosen the rib from the breast.

Grip the back portion in one hand and the breast portion in the other and pull apart. To halve the breast portion, lift the V-shaped side and divide by cutting down the middle bone, cracking it if necessary.

For the back portion, trim the end off and cut it in half, then divide the remaining portion down the middle by slicing, cracking the bone, then cutting through the flesh and skin. Trim off any bits of rib bone without skin.

## Tandoor

Tandoori dishes are, without doubt, the most celebrated of Indian dishes. This ancient method of cooking involves grilling traditional dishes and bread in a tandoor, which is a cylindrical clay oven that looks like a large, Alibaba pot. A blazing fire is lit inside it using wood or charcoal, and the tandoor is either surrounded by a square stone enclosure, or built into the ground.

The flavour of tandoori chicken, the standard tandoori speciality, surpasses any dish. Tender, spring chickens are marinated for at least 12 hours in fresh curds and spices. Special colouring imparts a red-gold colour to the chickens, which are then speared on long, thin spikes and placed in the tandoor, with the spikes resting on the oven's neck. The oven releases a mellow fragrance, because it is occasionally rubbed with a marinade made of mustard oil, spinach, molasses, salt and eggs. The flavour is also enhanced by the smoke rising from the marinade dripping onto the glowing coals.

Tandoori chicken is always accompanied by the tandoori bread known as naan. A piece of soft dough is patted into a flat disc by hand and thrust inside the tandoor. The outward, curving shape of the oven allows the greater part of the naan to hang loose over the heat, and the weight of the dough pulls the naan into its characteristic teardrop shape.

# SPICY BARBECUED CHICKEN | *MURGHI BRAAI*

*Although this recipe calls for marinated chicken pieces for the barbecue, you may use the same recipe for lamb chops.*

1.5 kg chicken pieces

MARINADE
30 ml (2 tbsp) cooking oil
5 ml (1 tsp) salt
5 ml (1 tsp) turmeric
3 ml (½ tsp) red masala
5 ml (1 tsp) green masala
5 ml (1 tsp) fresh garlic, pounded
8 ml (1½ tsp) fresh ginger, pounded
20 ml (4 tsp) lemon juice
90 ml (6 tbsp) melted butter for basting

Wash the chicken pieces and pat dry. Make a paste with the marinade ingredients and rub over the chicken pieces. Leave for 2 to 3 hours.

Prepare the coals for barbecuing. Place the chicken on a grill and cook slowly for about 20 minutes on each side, basting occasionally with melted butter.

Serve with lemon wedges, fresh salad and rolls.

**Time: 1 hour, plus 2 to 3 hours marinating**
**Serves 6**

# TANDOORI CHICKEN | *TANDOORI MURGHI*

*Tender spring chicken is used to make this roasted tandoori speciality with its distinctive rich, russet colour. The chicken is tenderised in a yoghurt marinade, seasoned with delicate spices.*

1 kg spring chicken
sprigs of dhania (coriander) to garnish

MARINADE
8 ml (1½ tsp) green masala
5 ml (1 tsp) salt
5 ml (1 tsp) fresh ginger, pounded
5 ml (1 tsp) fresh garlic, pounded
5 ml (1 tsp) turmeric
or 2 ml (¼ tsp) special tandoori colouring
30 ml (2 tbsp) ghee or cooking oil
15 ml (3 tbsp) dhania-jeero (coriander-cumin)
30 ml (2 tbsp) dhania (coriander) leaves, chopped
250 ml (1 cup) buttermilk or 125 ml (½ cup) cream

Split the chicken in two, cutting from the neck to the legs. Wash and pat dry. Combine the marinade ingredients and marinate the chicken for at least 5 hours, but preferably overnight.

Place the bird in an ovenproof dish and bake in an oven preheated to 180°C for 1 hour, then brown under the grill, basting with the juices. (Be careful, tandoori chicken has a tendency to dry out.)

Garnish with sprigs of coriander and serve with a salad and hot roti or fried rice. Apple chutney is a refreshing accompaniment. (As an alternative, garnish with tomato wedges and fried almonds.)

**Time: 1 hour, plus 5 hours marinating**
**Serves 4 to 6**

# BUTTER CHICKEN | *MAKHANI MURGHI*

1 kg skinless chicken fillets, washed
and cubed
80 ml ($\frac{1}{3}$ cup) ghee or margarine,
melted
3 tuj (cinnamon sticks), 5 cm each
1 large onion, grated
1 large ripe tomato
15 ml (1 tbsp) tomato paste
250 ml (1 cup) cream
dhania (coriander) leaves to garnish
5 ml (1 tsp) gharum masala to garnish

MARINADE
5 ml (1 tsp) salt
5 ml (1 tsp) turmeric
5 ml (1 tsp) red masala
3 ml (½ tsp) green masala
8 ml (1½ tsp) fresh ginger, pounded
5 ml (1 tsp) fresh garlic, pounded

Place the chicken pieces in a bowl. Mix together the marinade ingredients and rub well over the chicken pieces. Set aside for 30 minutes.

Heat the ghee in a flat saucepan and brown the cinnamon sticks for a few seconds. Add the onion and brown over a medium heat.

Add the chicken and stir well for 1 minute. Cover the saucepan and allow to cook over a low heat for 7 to 10 minutes, stirring occasionally to ensure that the chicken does not catch. Add the tomatoes, tomato paste and cream, then simmer for another 15 minutes.

Garnish with dhania leaves and serve on steamed basmati rice with fresh coconut chutney.

**Time: 30 minutes, plus 30 minutes marinating**
**Serves 6**

# STUFFED CHICKEN WITH SPICY RICE | *CHAVAL AUR MURGHI*

*Spices transform this chicken into a most elegant dish. The rice stuffing adds a touch of magic, while the rai and jeero create a delightful aroma. Traditionally baked in the clay tandoori oven, with the chicken skewered and a piece of dough stuck on the end of the skewer to keep it from slipping, the dish works well in a modern oven with the aid of foil. Serve the chicken with a crisp, green salad.*

1.5 kg chicken

MARINADE
3 ml (½ tsp) pepper
3 ml (½ tsp) gharum masala
5 ml (1 tsp) jeero (cumin seeds), crushed
30 ml (2 tbsp) melted butter
5 ml (1 tsp) salt

STUFFING
45 ml (3 tbsp) ghee or cooking oil
3 ml (½ tsp) jeero (cumin seeds)
3 ml (½ tsp) rai (mustard seeds)
1 onion, grated
3 ml (½ tsp) fresh ginger, pounded
3 ml (½ tsp) fresh garlic, pounded
500 ml (2 cups) cooked rice
1 large tomato, chopped
3 ml (½ tsp) salt

For the marinade, make a paste with the ingredients. Rub over the chicken and set aside for 3 hours.

To make the stuffing, heat the ghee in a saucepan. Add the jeero and rai, then brown for 20 seconds. Add the onion with the ginger and garlic and braise for 30 seconds. Add the rice, tomato and salt, stir for 2 minutes, then remove from the heat.

Preheat the oven to 180°C.

Stuff the chicken with the rice mixture. Cover with foil and bake for 60 minutes. Open the foil package and brown the chicken for 15 to 20 minutes. Serve on a warm platter.

**Time: 1¼ hours, plus 3 hours marinating**
**Serves 4**

# CHICKEN TIKKA | *TIKKA MURGHI*

*This Punjabi dish has become a firm favourite as it is so simple to prepare.*

500 g skinless chicken breasts, cubed
wooden skewers

MARINADE
125 ml (1 cup) low-fat yoghurt
10 ml (2 tsp) lemon juice
5 ml (1 tsp) gharum masala
5 ml (1 tsp) red chilli powder
5 ml (1 tsp) ginger, pounded
5 ml (1 tsp) garlic, pounded
5 ml (1 tsp) salt
3 ml (½ tsp) turmeric
10 ml (2 tsp) dhania-jeero
(coriander-cumin)
15 ml (1 tbsp) maizena
2 ml (¼ tsp) tandoori red colour powder

BASTING LIQUID
60 ml (4 tbsp) melted butter
5 ml (1 tsp) garlic, pounded

Wash the chicken pieces and pat dry. Mix the marinade ingredients in a bowl and rub over the chicken. Leave to stand overnight in the refrigerator.

Soak the skewers in water for a short while. Thread 4 to 6 chicken cubes onto each skewer and arrange on a baking tray. Place under a hot oven grill for 5 to 7 minutes. Remove from the oven and baste with the melted butter mixed with the garlic. Rotate the skewers and baste again. Return to the grill for a few minutes until brown. Pour over the leftover basting butter and serve hot.

VARIATION
Alternate the chicken pieces on the skewer with pineapple chunks, green and red peppers (capsicum), and onion. This makes a tasty and colourful kekaab stick.

This recipe may also be used for small chicken pieces on the bone, which are roasted over coals. Baste them regularly as they cook.

**Time: 30 minutes, plus overnight marinating**
**Serves 6**

Flame- or oven-grilled chicken tikka served
with peanut chutney and roti

# DRY CHICKEN CURRY | *KARHAI MURGHI*

*Perhaps this will bring a smile to many a seasoned cook while making this dish. When we were very young, our mothers used to urge us to eat more chicken by saying, 'Le dikhra Jireek chi chi Khaavo!' which translates to 'Come loved one, eat a little bit of chicken.'*

1 kg skinless chicken breasts, cut into bite-size pieces
60 ml (4 tbsp) ghee or margarine
2 large ripe tomatoes, grated
5 ml (1 tsp) gharum masala
30 ml (2 tbsp) chopped dhania (coriander) leaves

MARINADE
15 ml (1 tbsp) cooking oil
10 ml (2 tsp) lemon juice
5 ml (1 tsp) salt
5 ml (1 tsp) turmeric
5 ml (1 tsp) green masala
5 ml (1 tsp) red masala
5 ml (1 tsp) fresh ginger, pounded
5 ml (1 tsp) fresh garlic, pounded

Wash the chicken and place in a dish. Mix the marinade ingredients to a paste and rub over the chicken pieces. Leave to marinate for 30 minutes.

Heat the ghee in a large pan. Braise the marinated chicken for 7 to 10 minutes over a medium heat or until all moisture evaporates. Add the tomatoes and heat until the chicken is cooked through. Cover the pot with a lid and set aside.

Garnish with the gharum masala and dhania. Serve the chicken with hot roti.

**Time: 1 hour, plus 30 minutes marinating
Serves 4**

TIP
This chicken dish may be served as a snack accompaniment with cocktails. Pierce the pieces with toothpicks and garnish with hard-boiled eggs, cut into wedges. Pour the leftover tomato-chicken gravy over the eggs.

# CHICKEN CURRY | *MURGHI TARKHARI*

*This spicy marinated dish transforms ordinary chicken into a celebratory meal. It is redolent with the tantalising aroma of cinnamon, cloves and cardamom. Gem squashes are used to thicken the gravy.*

1.5 kg chicken, washed, skinned and cut into pieces

### MARINADE
5 ml (1 tsp) fresh ginger, pounded
5 ml (1 tsp) fresh garlic, pounded
15 ml (1 tbsp) salt
15 ml (1 tbsp) lemon juice
8 ml (1½ tsp) red masala
8 ml (1½ tsp) turmeric
15 ml (1 tbsp) cooking oil

### VAGAAR
60 ml (4 tbsp) cooking oil or ghee
6 lavang (whole cloves)
5 elachi (cardamom pods)
3 tuj (cinnamon sticks), 5 cm each
1½ onions, chopped
4 potatoes, halved
2 small gem squashes, peeled and diced
500 ml (2 cups) warm water
2 tomatoes, grated
5 ml (1 tsp) gharum masala
45 ml (3 tbsp) dhania (coriander) leaves, chopped

Mix together the marinade ingredients and rub the mixture well over the chicken pieces. Leave to marinate for at least 3 hours or overnight.

For the vagaar, heat the oil in a large saucepan. Add the lavang, elachi and tuj, and brown for 10 seconds. Add the onions and cook until golden brown. Stir in the chicken and braise for 10 minutes until well coated with the spices. Add the potatoes, gem squashes and the water. Cover the pot and cook for 30 minutes over a medium heat. Add the tomatoes and cook for a further 15 minutes.

Sprinkle gharum masala over the chicken and garnish with the dhania. Serve with white rice or hot roti, and a kachoomer (salad).

**Time: 1 hour, plus 3 hours marinating**
**Serves 6**

# FRIED CHICKEN | *TARELI MURGHI*

*This fried murghi is a succulent and delicately spiced chicken, absorbing the flavours of the onions and carrots, which remain firm. It is an impressive yet easy dish to prepare.*

1.5 kg chicken, cut into pieces
60 ml (4 tbsp) ghee or margarine
4 small onions
4 potatoes, halved
4 carrots, halved lengthwise
30 ml (2 tbsp) dhania (coriander) leaves, chopped

MARINADE
15 ml (1 tbsp) cooking oil
10 ml (2 tsp) lemon juice
8 ml (1½ tsp) salt
5 ml (1 tsp) turmeric
8 ml (1½ tsp) green masala
8 ml (1½ tsp) fresh ginger, pounded
8 ml (1½ tsp) fresh garlic, pounded

Wash the chicken and place in a dish. Mix the marinade ingredients to a paste, then rub over the chicken pieces. Leave to marinate for 30 minutes.

Heat the ghee in a large pan. Arrange the chicken and vegetables in the pan, cover and cook over a low heat for 30 to 40 minutes. Turn the chicken and vegetables and allow to brown over a higher heat for 10 to 12 minutes.

Garnish with the dhania and serve with hot roti or rolls, salad and a tomato or dhania chutney.

**Time: 1 hour, plus 30 minutes marinating**
**Serves 4**

Fried chicken and aromatic rice

# SPICY SCRAMBLED EGGS | *INDA NA POORA*

*Creamy scrambled egg, seasoned with the delicate flavour of dhania and a fresh chilli, is a Sunday morning favourite at my breakfast table. I serve it with grilled tomatoes topped with melted cheese, and hot foolka. Inda na poora is also delicious on toast as a snack or a quick light meal. If you prefer crunchy onions, add them to the raw eggs without first frying them.*

2 medium onions, chopped
60 ml (¼ cup) ghee or cooking oil
6 eggs
3 ml (½ tsp) green masala
5 ml (1 tsp) salt
30 ml (2 tbsp) dhania (coriander) leaves, chopped
3 ml (½ tsp) turmeric
5 ml (1 tsp) dhania-jeero (coriander-cumin)
3 ml (½ tsp) gharum masala

Fry the onions in ghee in a large pan until golden brown.

Whisk the eggs and spices well in a bowl, then add to the onions in the pan. Stir, allowing to cook until set but still soft.

**Time: 15 minutes**
**Serves 4**

# SPINACH & EGG SCRAMBLE | *BHAJI INDA NU SAKH*

*This is ideal as an emergency meal, or a quick snack served on toast. It also makes a good filling for toasted sandwiches.*

200 g (1 bunch) spinach or 3 bunches methi (fenugreek)
60 ml (¼ cup) cooking oil or ghee
2 onions, sliced
2 ml (¼ tsp) turmeric
5 ml (1 tsp) dhania-jeero (coriander-cumin)
5 ml (1 tsp) gharum masala
5 ml (1 tsp) green masala
6 eggs, beaten
3 ml (½ tsp) salt

Wash the spinach well, then chop it finely. (If you are using methi, cut off the roots and thicker stems, wash well and chop finely.)

Heat the oil in a saucepan and fry the onions until brown. Stir in the spinach. Add the spices and cook for 10 minutes until the moisture evaporates.

Season the eggs with salt and pour over the spinach. Stir until set (not more than 5 minutes). The eggs should remain soft.

This dish may be reheated over a low heat.

**Time: 15 minutes**
**Serves 4**

# SPICY EGG-FRIED BREAD | *INDA FRIED BREAD*

*Try these slices of bread coated with a crisp layer of spiced egg for a delightful breakfast, light meal or snack.*

4 eggs
3 ml (½ tsp) salt
3 ml (½ tsp) green masala
3 ml (½ tsp) turmeric
15 ml (1 tbsp) dhania (coriander) leaves, chopped
15 ml (1 tbsp) dhania-jeero (coriander-cumin)
4 slices bread
60 ml (4 tbsp) ghee or oil for shallow frying

Place the eggs in a bowl. Whisk well with the salt and spices.
  Dip the bread slices into the egg mixture. Over a medium heat, fry the slices on both sides until golden.

**Time: 15 minutes**
**Serves 4**

# MINCE CURRY | *KHIMA TARKHARI*

*Basic spices elevate humble mince into a richly flavoured dish.*

1 kg mutton mince or chicken mince
250 ml (1 cup) cold water
10 ml (2 tsp) salt
10 ml (2 tsp) fresh garlic, pounded
13 ml (2½ tsp) fresh ginger, pounded
5 ml (1 tsp) green masala
5 ml (1 tsp) turmeric
10 ml (2 tsp) lemon juice

### VAGAAR
80 ml (⅓ cup) cooking oil
2 tuj (cinnamon sticks), 5 cm each
4 lavang (whole cloves)
4 elachi (cardamom pods)
2 onions, chopped
4 potatoes, halved
4 carrots, halved
2 tomatoes, grated or chopped
30 ml (2 tbsp) dhania (coriander) leaves, chopped
5 ml (1 tsp) gharum masala

In a large bowl, break up the mince thoroughly with your fingers. Add the water and stir to break up further (the water will evaporate while cooking). Mix in the salt, garlic, ginger, masala, turmeric and lemon juice.

To make the vagaar, heat the oil and spices in a large saucepan with a well-fitting lid. Add the onions, cover, reduce the heat and allow the onions to brown. Add the mince and braise for 5 to 7 minutes. Stir in the potatoes and carrots, then cover and cook for 30 minutes over a medium heat. Stir occasionally. Add the tomatoes, cover and cook for a further 10 minutes.

Garnish with the dhania and gharum masala. Serve with warm roti, foolka bread or naan, and a dhania chutney.

**Time: 1 hour**
**Serves 6**

# EASY BAKED MINCE | *BHOPTO*

500 g chicken mince
5 ml (1 tsp) salt
5 ml (1 tsp) red masala
5 ml (1 tsp) fresh ginger, pounded
5 ml (1 tsp) fresh garlic, pounded
5 ml (1 tsp) turmeric
10 ml (2 tbsp) fresh dhania
(coriander) leaves, chopped
10 ml (2 tbsp) ghee
2 eggs, whisked
lettuce leaves for lining dish

Preheat the oven to 180°C.

Mix together all the ingredients (except the lettuce). Line a small, ovenproof dish with the lettuce leaves and carefully spoon in the mixture. Bake for about 30 minutes, until firm. Cut into squares and serve with chutney.

**Time: 30 minutes**
**Serves 6**

# MINCE BALLS | *KHIMA KEBAAB*

*These mince balls are cooked in a cinnamon-enriched tomato gravy.*

500 g chicken or lamb mince
5 ml (1 tsp) green masala
5 ml (1 tsp) turmeric
5 ml (1 tsp) fresh ginger, pounded
5 ml (1 tsp) fresh garlic, pounded
3 ml (½ tsp) gharum masala
1 small onion, grated
10 ml (2 tsp) lemon juice
30 ml (2 tbsp) dhania (coriander)
leaves, chopped
30 ml (2 tbsp) cooking oil
2 tuj (cinnamon sticks), 5 cm each
2 tomatoes, grated

Mix together the mince, green masala, turmeric, ginger, garlic, gharum masala, onion, lemon juice and 1 T dhania. Roll the mixture into small balls in the palms of your hands.

Heat the oil in a pot, add the cinnamon and brown. Add the mince balls to the pot, cover and cook over a low heat for 20 minutes. Add the tomatoes and cook for a further 10 minutes.

Garnish with the remaining dhania. Serve with foolka or hot roti and dhania or tomato chutney.

**Time: 30 minutes**
**Serves 4**

# BARBECUED MINCE BALLS | *SEEKH KEBAAB*

*Seekh kebaab originates from the royal cuisine of the Moghul emperors who invaded India in the 16th century. The mouth-watering flavour is the result of a perfect balance of spices and the use of a covered coal barbecue. Use Indian skewers or seekhs, made of key steel and at least 75 cm long. They are squared to 6 mm thickness to prevent the kebaabs from falling off during barbecuing. Securing the kebaabs on these unusual skewers is an art in itself. Fatty meat is essential, as it helps to bind the kebaabs.*

2.5 kg fatty lamb or mutton mince
30 ml (2 tbsp) green masala
20 ml (4 tsp) fresh garlic, pounded
25 ml (5 tsp) fresh ginger, pounded
13 ml (2½ tsp) salt
10 ml (2 tsp) turmeric
45 ml (3 tbsp) lemon juice
250 ml (1 cup) dhania (coriander) leaves
2 onions, grated (squeeze out excess juice)

Mix together all the ingredients and shape into small, walnut-sized balls. Carefully thread 12 kebaabs closely onto each skewer. Secure the kebaabs by pressing them tightly onto the skewer with the palm of your hand. It should resemble one long kebaab.

Barbecue the kebaabs over red coals for approximately 10 to 12 minutes, rotating the skewers from time to time. Avoid flames by sprinkling cold water over the coals. The kebaabs turn golden brown when done.

Serve two kebaabs at a time on foolka bread and top with their essential accompaniment, dhania chutney.

**Time: 2 hours, including braai time**
**Serves 8 to 10**

# MINCE WITH PEAS & MINT | *KHIMA AUR MATAR*

ingredients as per Khima
Tarkhari (page 84)
500 ml (2 cups) frozen peas
45 ml (3 tbsp) fresh mint, chopped

Add the peas and mint to the basic mince mixture 15 minutes before the end of cooking but only after the tomatoes have been added and cooked for 10 minutes.

**Time: 1 hour**
**Serves 6**

# GREEN PEPPERS STUFFED WITH MINCE |
## *BHARELA KHIMA MIRCHA*

*Serve these stuffed green peppers with pilau or warm roti, and a salad or chutney.*
*For an exotic variation, replace the green peppers with baby brinjals.*

6 green peppers (capsicum)
500 g chicken or lamb mince
60 ml (4 tbsp) ghee or cooking oil
2 medium onions, finely grated or
chopped in a processor
5 ml (1 tsp) green masala
5 ml (1 tsp) salt
3 ml (½ tsp) turmeric
3 ml (½ tsp) dhania (coriander)
seeds, crushed
8 ml (1½ tsp) fresh ginger, pounded
5 ml (1 tsp) fresh garlic, pounded
2 tomatoes, grated
30 ml (2 tbsp) dhania (coriander) leaves,
chopped, to garnish

Slit the green peppers in quarters lengthwise, keeping the base intact.

Mix the mince with 1 T ghee, the onions, spices and garlic. Stuff the peppers with the mince mixture.

Heat the remaining ghee in a heavy saucepan. Arrange the peppers in the pan, then cook, covered, over a medium to low heat for 45 minutes.

Add the tomatoes, then garnish with the dhania leaves. Serve as described above.

**Time: 1 hour**
**Serves 4**

# MUTTON CURRY | *GOSHT TARKHARI*

*Mutton curry with rice is a favourite and perhaps the most renowned Indian dish. Brinjals (or cubed gem squash) are used to thicken the tarkhari, which is served with rice and kachoomer (salad).*

1 kg mutton pieces (any cut)
200 g (1 medium) brinjal,
peeled and cubed
500 ml (2 cups) hot water
4 potatoes, peeled and halved
2 large ripe tomatoes, grated
5 ml (1 tsp) gharum masala
30 ml (2 tbsp) dhania (coriander)
leaves, chopped

### MARINADE
15 ml (1 tbsp) cooking oil
8 ml (1½ tsp) red masala
5 ml (1 tsp) salt
10 ml (2 tsp) fresh ginger, pounded
5 ml (1 tsp) turmeric
5 ml (1 tsp) lemon juice

### VAGAAR
60 ml (4 tbsp) cooking oil
3 tuj (cinnamon sticks), 5 cm each
6 lavang (whole cloves)
4 elachi (cardamom pods)
2 onions, chopped

Wash the mutton. Mix together the marinade ingredients and rub into the mutton. Set aside for 30 minutes.

To make the vagaar, heat the oil in a saucepan. Add the spices and onions, then brown.

In the same pan, braise the meat and brinjal cubes for 10 minutes. Add the water, cover and simmer on a medium heat for 45 minutes. Add the potatoes, stir and cook for another 20 minutes. Stir in the tomatoes and cook for a further 10 minutes.

Garnish with gharum masala and dhania leaves. Serve with a helping of steaming white rice.

**Time: 1 hour 45 minutes**
**Serves 6**

# LAMB & LENTIL CURRY | *GOSHT DHAL*

*Succulent morsels of lamb simmered in a rich, thick gravy of lentils provides an excellent dish for a cold winter's night. Serve over a helping of rice, with a fresh kachoomer (salad). A chicken may be substituted for the lamb.*

375 ml (1½ cups) oil dhal or toover dhal
1 kg lamb or mutton pieces (any cut)
30 ml (2 tbsp) cooking oil
5 ml (1 tsp) red masala
5 ml (1 tsp) fresh garlic, pounded
10 ml (2 tsp) fresh ginger, pounded
8 ml (1½ tsp) turmeric
10 ml (2 tsp) salt
45 ml (3 tbsp) dhania (coriander) leaves, chopped
5 ml (1 tsp) gharum masala (optional)

VAGAAR
45 ml (3 tbsp) cooking oil
5 whole elachi (cardamom pods)
3 tuj (cinnamon sticks), 5 cm each
5 lavang (whole cloves)
2 medium onions, chopped

Pick over, then soak the oil dhal (or toover dhal) in warm water and leave for 30 minutes. Wash the meat. Mix together the oil, red masala, garlic, ginger, turmeric and salt, and rub well over the meat.

To make the vagaar, heat the oil in a large saucepan, then add the elachi (still whole), tuj and lavang. Fry for 20 seconds, then add the onions and cover the pan. Reduce to a medium heat and allow the onions to brown.

Add the meat and braise for 5 to 7 minutes. Gradually add up to 3 C warm water as well as the drained oil dhal and leave to simmer over a medium heat until the meat has cooked. This should take approximately 90 minutes. Stir during cooking to ensure that the dhal does not catch at the base of the pan. At this stage the dhal should resemble a full-bodied gravy, not too thick.

Garnish with dhania leaves and gharum masala. Serve with steamed basmati rice.

**Time: 1½ to 2 hours**
**Serves 6**

# SWEET-SOUR LAMB CUBES | *KHATTI MITTHI GOSHT BOTI*

*The two compatible opposites, vinegar and sugar, make a pleasing combination in this tantalising meat dish.*
*A scattering of crisp potato strips elevates this dish to royal fare. If you need to freeze the dish, omit the potato strips.*

1 kg lamb, cubed
8 ml (1½ tsp) salt
5 ml (1 tsp) turmeric
60 ml (4 tbsp) cooking oil
6 lavang (whole cloves)
2 tuj (cinnamon sticks), 4 cm each
6 peppercorns
2 large onions, chopped
10 ml (2 tsp) red masala
10 ml (2 tsp) fresh garlic, pounded
10 ml (2 tsp) fresh ginger, pounded
10 ml (2 tsp) dhania-jeero
(coriander-cumin)
125 ml (½ cup) brown vinegar
30 ml (2 tbsp) sugar

POTATO STRIPS
2 large potatoes, peeled and grated
cooking oil for deep frying

Wash the lamb cubes, pat dry and sprinkle with salt and turmeric. Set aside.

Heat the oil in a heavy saucepan. Add the lavang, tuj and peppercorns, then brown for 10 seconds. Add the onions and braise until a golden colour.

Still on a medium heat, add the red masala, garlic, ginger, dhania-jeero and 4 tsp water, and fry well for 3 to 5 minutes, until the oil rises to the surface.

Add the lamb cubes and braise for 5 minutes. Add 1 cup water, cover the saucepan and cook over a low heat for 35 minutes, until the lamb is tender. More water may be added when necessary.

Mix together the vinegar and sugar, then add to the lamb. Cover the saucepan and cook for 10 minutes.

While the meat is cooking, prepare the potato strips. Wash the grated potatoes and dry with absorbent paper, removing as much moisture as possible. Heat the oil for deep frying and fry 2 tbsp potato at a time, until golden and crispy. Drain once more on absorbent paper.

Serve the lamb in a large bowl with the potato strips sprinkled over the top.

**Time: 1 hour**
**Serves 6**

# CABBAGE & MUTTON CURRY | *KHUBI GOSHT TARKHARI*

*In this dish, the tasty mutton flavour is readily absorbed by the cabbage and potatoes.*
*The three combine to make a mouth-watering tarkhari, best served with long grain rice and a beetroot salad.*

1 kg mutton, cut into pieces
8 ml (1½ tsp) red masala
8 ml (1½ tsp) turmeric
10 ml (2 tsp) salt
5 ml (1 tsp) fresh garlic, pounded
10 ml (2 tsp) fresh ginger, pounded
15 ml (1 tbsp) cooking oil

VAGAAR
45 ml (3 tbsp) cooking oil
3 tuj (cinnamon sticks), 5 cm each
6 lavang (whole cloves)
4 elachi (cardamom pods) (optional)
2 onions, chopped
750 ml (3 cups) warm water
6 potatoes, halved
1 small cabbage (approx. 400 g),
shredded
2 tomatoes, grated (for pulp)
8 ml (1½ tsp) gharum masala
30 ml (2 tbsp) dhania (coriander) leaves,
chopped

Wash the mutton and arrange in a dish. Mix together the masala, turmeric, salt, garlic, ginger and oil, then combine well with the meat.

For the vagaar, heat the oil in a large saucepan, add the tuj, lavang and elachi, then brown for 10 seconds. Stir in the onions and fry until golden brown, then increase the heat to high and braise the meat in the mixture for 10 minutes. Pour in the water, cover and simmer for 45 minutes on a medium heat. Add the potatoes and cabbage, and cook, covered until they are soft. Finally, add the tomatoes and cook for a further 10 minutes.

Sprinkle with gharum masala and garnish with dhania leaves.

**Time: 1½ hours**
**Serves 6 to 8**

# ROAST LAMB | RAAN MASALA

*This spiced leg of lamb is roasted in heavy foil. Serve it with fried rice or mushroom pilau, golden roast potatoes and dhania chutney.*

2 kg leg of lamb
5 ml (1 tsp) turmeric
8 ml (1½ tsp) red masala
8 ml (1½ tsp) salt
10 ml (2 tsp) fresh ginger, pounded
5 ml (1 tsp) fresh garlic, pounded
30 ml (2 tbsp) cooking oil
8 to 10 lavang (whole cloves)

Wash and wipe the meat well.

Make a paste of the turmeric, masala, salt, ginger, garlic and oil. Rub the paste well over the leg. Finally, stud the leg with the cloves and allow to marinate overnight or for a few hours.

Wrap the meat in a sheet of heavy foil and roast in an oven preheated to 160°C for 2 hours, allowing 30 minutes for every 500 g meat used. Open the foil wrapper and bake for a further 20 to 30 minutes, basting frequently with the cooking liquid.

**Time: 2½ hours, plus overnight marinating**
**Serves 6 to 8**

# SPICY EGG-FRIED CHOPS | *INDA GOSHT BOTI*

*The unsurpassed flavour of these rich, tender chops with a spicy coating, make for a special dinner party dish. Serve them with golden roast potatoes, warm roti and a vegetable curry.*

1 kg lamb chops
500 ml (2 cups) water
10 ml (2 tsp) salt
13 ml (2½ tsp) green masala
5 ml (1 tsp) fresh ginger, pounded
5 ml (1 tsp) fresh garlic, pounded
5 eggs
3 ml (½ tsp) turmeric
5 ml (1 tsp) dhania-jeero (coriander-cumin)
3 ml (½ tsp) gharum masala
30 ml (2 tbsp) dhania (coriander) leaves, chopped
80 ml (⅓ cup) ghee or cooking oil for shallow frying

Wash the chops and place them in a pot with the water. Add 1½ t each of the salt and green masala, as well as the ginger and garlic. Simmer for 30 to 40 minutes, until the chops are cooked.

In a bowl, whisk together the eggs, the remaining salt and green masala, turmeric, dhania-jeero, gharum masala and dhania leaves, until fluffy.

Heat the ghee in a frying pan. Coat the chops well by dipping each into the egg mixture. Fry them on both sides for 2 to 3 minutes over a medium heat until golden brown.

**Time: 1 hour**
**Serves 6**

# LAMB MASALA CHOPS | *SHAHI GOSHT KORMA*

*I prefer using the neat loin cuts for this popular northern Indian dish, which is tenderised in a yoghurt marinade, seasoned with ginger and garlic. If you like, use more saffron as it is this that gives the dish its superb flavour. The dish may also be prepared as a snack for cocktails. Serve it with a fresh mint or dhania chutney, or with onion rings soaked in lemon juice.*

500 g mutton or lamb chops (lamb cooks more quickly)
5 ml (1 tsp) green masala
3 ml (½ tsp) red masala
5 ml (1 tsp) dhania-jeero (coriander-cumin)
8 ml (1½ tsp) fresh ginger, pounded
5 ml (1 tsp) fresh garlic, pounded
3 ml (½ tsp) turmeric
5 ml (1 tsp) salt
250 ml (1 cup) yoghurt
15 threads (1 tsp) saffron
45 ml (3 tbsp) dhania (coriander) leaves
125 ml (½ cup) cooking oil
2 onions, sliced

Wash the chops and rub well with the masalas, dhania-jeero, ginger, garlic, turmeric and salt.

Pour the yoghurt over, add the saffron threads and sprinkle with half the dhania leaves. Leave to stand for 2 hours.

Heat the oil in a flat, covered saucepan. Add the onions and fry until soft. Add the masala chops to the pan and simmer for 45 to 60 minutes until tender. During cooking, ½ cup water may be added if necessary. The chops should have little or no gravy. Garnish with the remaining dhania leaves.

**Time: 80 minutes, plus 2 hours marinating**
**Serves 2 to 3**

# MUTTON CHOPS WITH GREEN BEANS | *PAPADI GOSHT TARKHARI*

*In this dish, mutton chops are prepared with French beans and whole tomatoes. The chops cook to a dry tarkhari that is succulent and superb. Serve with warm roti and fresh salad. A rice dish would also be an appropriate accompaniment.*

1 kg mutton chops
5 ml (1 tsp) red chilli powder or red masala
10 ml (2 tsp) fresh ginger, pounded
5 ml (1 tsp) fresh garlic, pounded
15 ml (1 tbsp) dhania (coriander) seeds, crushed
5 ml (1 tsp) salt
5 ml (1 tsp) turmeric
125 ml (½ cup) cooking oil
2 tuj (cinnamon sticks), 5 cm each
4 elachi (cardamom pods)
375 ml (1½ cups) warm water
500 g French beans, topped and tailed
4 small ripe tomatoes
4 small onions, peeled and halved
5 ml (1 tsp) gharum masala
30 ml (2 tbsp) dhania (coriander) leaves, chopped

Wash the chops and pat dry. Add the chilli powder, ginger, garlic, dhania seeds, salt and turmeric.

Heat the oil in a saucepan, add the tuj and elachi, then brown gently for a few minutes.

Add the chops and brown for 5 minutes on either side. Add the water and cook, covered, for 45 minutes until tender.

Arrange the beans, tomatoes and onions in-between the chops. Cover and cook for another 15 minutes until tender.

Garnish with the gharum masala and coriander leaves.

**Time: 1½ hours**
**Serves 4 to 6**

Delicious mutton chops with green beans and whole tomatoes served with roti and mushroom & cashew nut curry

# Fish & Seafood

*Fishing is a way of life in coastal India. At daybreak, thousands of fishermen steer their antiquated boats serenely through the morning mist. Long nets haul in shoals of sardines, pomfret, mackerel and small sharks.*

*Superb prawns, crabs, mussels, oysters, squid and clams are harvested on the southern coast.*

*In the fish market, robust fishwives shout their prices to the villagers. Fish curry and rice is everyday fare in the coastal communities. On the tropical south coast, fish is marinated in tamarind juice and coconut milk, spiced and wrapped in layers of banana leaves. Folded and tied into a square, the wrapped fish is gently roasted over hot ash, preserving the liquid and ensuring an unsurpassed flavour.*

*In Mumbai the fisherman's speciality is still the slender bony fish called Bombay duck. Heaps of this long fish lie about on the beaches and streets, drying to tough sticks resembling biltong. The overpowering smell explains why Bombay duck is not the most popular fish in Indian cuisine, though the locals transform this malodorous delicacy into a tantalising side dish or pickle.*

# GRILLED FISH | *MASALA TAMATI MACHI*

*This delectable grilled fish is best served over steaming yellow khitcheri (rice) or with mashed potatoes.*
*Any type of fish may be used.*

1 kg fresh fish, filleted and sliced
2 medium tomatoes, sliced
2 medium onions, cut into rings

MARINADE
5 ml (1 tsp) red masala
15 ml (3 tsp) dhania-jeero
(coriander-cumin)
5 ml (1 tsp) fresh garlic, pounded
5 ml (1 tsp) turmeric
15 ml (1 tbsp) lemon juice
30 ml (2 tbsp) cooking oil
10 ml (2 tsp) salt
30 ml (2 tbsp) dhania (coriander)
leaves, chopped

Wash the fish and dry with absorbent paper.

Combine the marinade ingredients and rub the paste over the slices of fish. Place in an ovenproof dish and leave to marinate for 1 to 2 hours.

Regularly basting with the marinade, cook the fish under a grill for 7 minutes. Add the tomatoes and onions and grill for a further 7 minutes or until the vegetables are soft.

Serve with rice or mashed potato, a tossed salad, rolls and pickles.

**Time: 20 minutes, plus 2 hours marinating**
**Serves 6**

Succulent grilled hake served with
spicy mash and vegetables

# SIMPLE GRILLED FISH | *MASALA MACHI*

*This dish, with its delicate flavour, was a winner at my restaurant.*

1 kg whole hake fillet (with skin)
10 ml (2 tsp) fresh garlic, pounded
5 ml (1 tsp) salt
5 ml (1 tsp) red chilli powder or paprika
juice of half a lemon
45 ml (3 tbsp) melted ghee

Arrange the length of the fish in an ovenproof dish (do not cut it into pieces). Sprinkle with the garlic, salt and chilli powder (add more if you like), then squeeze over the lemon juice. Finally, pour the ghee over the fish.

Bake in the oven under a hot grill for 10 minutes.

Serve with steamed vegetables and steamed basmati rice.

**Time: 20 minutes**
**Serves 6**

# BAKED FISH | *MACHI*

60 ml (4 tbsp) tomato sauce (or tomato paste with 10 ml (2 tsp) sugar)
1 kg fresh fish fillets
2 tomatoes, sliced
1 red onion, sliced
a few strips green and yellow peppers

Preheat the oven to 180°C.

Use the same marinade as per Grilled Fish (top). Add the tomato sauce to the marinade. Cover the fish with the marinade and marinate for at least 2 hours.

Transfer the fish to a large greased ovenproof dish. Neatly arrange the vegetables over the top and bake for 35 minutes.

Serve with rolls or rotis and salad.

**Time: 45 minutes**
**Serves 6**

# FISH FILLETS IN BATTER | *MACHI PAKORA*

*Pakora is popular in India. The spicy batter is made from lentil flour, although self-raising flour may be substituted.*

500 g fish fillets
3 ml (½ tsp) fresh garlic, pounded
8 ml (1½ tsp) salt
250 ml (1 cup) chana flour or
self-raising flour
3 ml (½ tsp) baking powder
8 ml (1½ tsp) dhania-jeero
(coriander-cumin)
3 ml (½ tsp) green masala
3 ml (½ tsp) chilli powder or paprika
2 ml (¼ tsp) turmeric
30 ml (2 tbsp) dhania (coriander) leaves,
chopped
250 ml (1 cup) water
750 ml (3 cup) cooking oil for deep
frying

Cut the fillets into 2.5 cm squares, wash and pat dry. Rub the garlic and 1 t salt well over the fish. Leave to stand for 15 minutes. Sift the flour into a bowl with the baking powder. Mix in the remaining salt, the dhania-jeero, masala, chilli powder, turmeric, dhania leaves and water to form a creamy batter.

Heat the oil in a deep saucepan. Dip each fillet in the batter and fry for 3 minutes on either side until golden brown. Drain on absorbent paper and serve immediately with lemon wedges and a fresh chutney.

**Time: 40 minutes, plus 15 minutes marinating**
**Serves 2 to 4**

# FRIED OR BARBECUED FISH | *TARELI MACHI*

1 kg fresh firm fish, cut into pieces
oil for shallow frying or
60 ml (4 tbsp) butter for barbecuing

MARINADE
5 ml (1 tsp) green masala
5 ml (1 tsp) red masala
3 ml (½ tsp) gharum masala
15 ml (1 tbsp) dhania-jeero
(coriander-cumin)
10 ml (2 tsp) fresh garlic, pounded
5 ml (1 tsp) fresh ginger, pounded
8 ml (1½ tsp) turmeric
10 ml (2 tsp) salt
15 ml (1 tbsp) lemon juice
125 ml (½ cup) cooking oil

Wash the fish and pat dry. Make a paste of the marinade ingredients and rub over the fish pieces. Leave to marinate for at least 2 hours.

Fry the fish in shallow oil over medium heat until golden brown on both sides (about 5 minutes). Alternatively, to barbecue the fish, place on a grill over the coals and baste on both sides with butter.

Serve with hot roti and wedges of lemon, moong lentils and a potato fry.

**Time: 1 hour, plus 2 hours marinating**
**Serves 6**

# STUFFED BRINJAL & DRIED SHRIMP CURRY | SAULA BARELA VENGRA

*Like Bombay duck, dried shrimps are a food for the Indian gourmet.*

200 g dried shrimps, soaked in warm
water for 2 hours
60 ml (¼ cup) cooking oil
5 ml (1 tsp) jeero (cumin seeds)
5 ml (1 tsp) methi (fenugreek) seeds
2 large onions, chopped
60 ml (¼ cup) dhania (coriander)
leaves, chopped
1 small tomato, grated
3 ml (½ tsp) salt
5 ml (1 tsp) green masala
5 ml (1 tsp) fresh garlic, pounded
5 ml (1 tsp) turmeric
15 ml (1 tbsp) dhania-jeero
(coriander-cumin)
3 ml (½ tsp) gharum masala
10 ml (2 tsp) sugar
3 potatoes, sliced
250 g baby brinjals
15 ml (1 tbsp) dhania (coriander)
leaves, chopped

The dried shrimps will expand after soaking. De-vein them and rinse well.

Heat the oil in a saucepan, and add the jeero and methi seeds. After 1 minute, add the shrimps and all other ingredients except the potatoes, brinjals and dhania leaves. Cook for 10 to 12 minutes.

Slit the brinjals from centre to bottom, without cutting right through. Stuff them well, using all the shrimp mixture. Arrange in the same saucepan, with the potatoes around the brinjals. Sprinkle with extra salt and dhania leaves. Cover and cook over a low heat for 45 minutes.

Serve with hot roti, or khudi and khitcheri, mango pickle and papadums.

**Time: 1¼ hours, plus 2 hours soaking**
**Serves 6**

# BAKED FISH IN BANANA LEAVES | *MADRASI PATRA NI MACHI*

*Southern India excels in its fish cuisine. Fresh coconut, tamarind and spices distinguish this dish, which is served on a banana leaf with a heap of steaming white rice. In true southern Indian style, the fish is hot and spicy, so go easy on the chillies if you prefer a milder dish.*

1 kg fresh fish pieces)
1 large banana leaf or a few spinach or cabbage leaves
string for tying leaves

MARINADE
30 ml (2 tbsp) vinegar or tamarind juice
½ fresh coconut, finely grated or chopped in a food processor
10 ml (2 tsp) salt
30 ml (2 tbsp) lemon juice
10 ml (2 tsp) sugar
10 ml (2 tsp) chilli powder
2 green chillies, finely chopped or 10 ml (2 tsp) green masala
15 ml (1 tbsp) jeero (cumin seeds), roasted and finely crushed
13 ml (2½ tsp) fresh garlic, pounded
45 ml (3 tbsp) dhania (coriander) leaves, chopped
45 ml (3 tbsp) cooking oil

Wash the fish well and pat dry. (To make tamarind juice for the marinade, soak 30 g tamarind in ¼ cup cold water, remove the seeds and strain.) Combine the marinade ingredients and coat the fish pieces. Marinate for 1 to 2 hours.

Tear the banana leaf (or spinach leaves) into smaller pieces. Wrap each piece of fish in a piece of leaf, tie with string and arrange on a baking tray. Sprinkle with a little water. Bake for 25 minutes in the centre of an oven preheated to 180°C. The texture of the fish should be soft and moist.

**Time: 40 minutes, plus 1 to 2 hours marinating**
**Serves 6 to 8**

Baked fish in banana leaves served with golden potatoes, coconut chutney, mango pickle and naan

# TANGY GRILLED PRAWNS | *KHATTA MITTHA JINGA*

*Serve these tangy prawns with a mushroom or kesar (saffron)-flavoured pilau and a crisp salad with a creamy dressing. The fresh green chillies impart a special flavour, but if they're unavailable, use a green masala instead.*

500 g prawns
60 ml (¼ cup) vinegar
30 ml (2 tbsp) ghor (sugar jaggery)
(or substitute golden syrup)
2 to 3 ripe tomatoes, grated
1 onion, grated or finely chopped
1 green chilli, finely chopped
2 ml (¼ tsp) red masala
10 ml (2 tsp) fresh garlic, pounded
3 ml (½ tsp) turmeric
5 ml (1 tsp) dhania-jeero (coriander-cumin)
45 ml (3 tbsp) dhania (coriander) leaves, chopped
2 ml (¼ tsp) salt
30 ml (2 tbsp) cooking oil

Clean the prawns by gently pinching and pulling off the tail shell and removing the claws. De-vein the prawns and wash under cold, running water.

Heat the vinegar in a small saucepan and dissolve the ghor. Leave to cool. In a bowl, make a thick sauce by mixing the rest of the ingredients well. Add the vinegar mixture and stir. Stir the prawns into the sauce, arrange on a baking tray and cover. Leave to stand for 1 hour.

Grill the prawns in their sauce for 7 minutes. Stir, then allow to brown for 10 minutes. The sauce should coat the prawns, so do not over-grill them.

**Time: 40 minutes, plus 1 hour marinating**
**Serves 2**

# FISH CURRY | *MACHI KARI*

*Fresh fish coated with a hot spicy marinade remains succulent as it simmers in rich tomato gravy, ideal for ladling over piping hot rice. Use any firm fish. Crayfish or prawns make an excellent substitute.*

1 kg fresh fish pieces or fillets
30 ml (2 tbsp) dhania (coriander)
leaves, chopped

### MARINADE
45 ml (3 tbsp) cooking oil
10 ml (2 tsp) salt
8 ml (1½ tsp) turmeric
5 ml (1 tsp) fresh ginger, pounded
5 ml (1 tsp) fresh garlic, pounded
15 ml (1 tbsp) dhania-jeero
(coriander-cumin)
10 ml (2 tsp) red masala
20 ml (4 tsp) lemon juice
10 limri (curry leaves)
15 ml (1 tbsp) dhania (coriander)
leaves, chopped

### GRAVY
70 g can tomato paste
or 425 g can whole tomatoes
10 ml (2 tsp) sugar
45 ml (3 tbsp) chana flour
250 ml (1 cup) cold water

### VAGAAR
45 ml (3 tbsp) cooking oil
2 green chillies, sliced lengthwise
5 ml (1 tsp) fresh garlic, pounded
5 ml (1 tsp) methi (fenugreek) seeds
1 large onion, finely chopped

Wash the fish and pat dry. Mix the marinade ingredients into a thick paste. Coat the fish well. Marinate for at least 3 hours or overnight.

For the gravy, place the tomato paste and sugar in a bowl. Slowly mix in the flour and water to make a thick paste.

For the vagaar, heat the oil in a large, flat pot, then add the spices. Stir in the onion and brown. Add the gravy mixture and cook, covered, over a medium heat for 15 minutes.

Add the fish and marinade to the pot, cover and cook for 10 to 20 minutes until the fish is done. Do not overcook.

**Time: 30 minutes, plus 3 hours marinating**
**Serves 6**

### VARIATIONS
Still using the recipe above, for a Royal Prawn Curry, use 1 kg of king (or queen) prawns in place of the fish pieces. For a Seafood Curry, replace the fish pieces with 500 g prawns, 250 g fish, 125 g calamari strips and 8 well-washed mussels.

# GOAN SEAFOOD CURRY | *JINGA AUR MACHI KARI*

*The town of Goa on the east coast of India adds its charm to Indian cuisine with its Portuguese influence.*

500 g tiger prawns
250 g firm fish
6 crayfish tails
5 ml (1 tsp) salt
5 ml (1 tsp) turmeric
5 ml (1 tsp) paprika (or chilli powder)
5 ml (1 tsp) lemon juice
5 ml (1 tsp) cooking oil
45 ml (3 tbsp) fresh coconut, finely
grated (or
2 T desiccated coconut)
250 ml (1 cup) warm water
6 large ripe tomatoes, skinned
45 ml (3 tbsp) ghee
30 ml (2 tbsp) cooking oil
2 large onions, finely chopped
10 ml (2 tsp) fresh garlic, pounded
5 ml (1 tsp) fresh ginger, pounded
5 ml (1 tsp) salt
10 limri (curry leaves)
5 ml (1 tsp) red chilli powder or paprika
3 ml (½ tsp) turmeric
1 to 2 green chillies, sliced lengthwise
5 ml (1 tsp) soomph (aniseed), crushed
10 ml (2 tsp) sugar
45 ml (3 tbsp) dhania (coriander)
leaves, chopped
30 ml (2 tbsp) tomato paste
250 ml (1 cup) coconut cream or
fresh cream

Prepare the seafood by rinsing the prawns in cold water. Remove the heads and pinch off the claws. De-vein the prawns to remove the dark dorsal vein. Cut the fish into 5 cm pieces, sprinkle with salt and wash with cold water. Clean the crayfish tails similarly and de-vein them. Leave the bright shells on, but larger tails may be cut in half if preferred. Place the seafood in a bowl and rub in salt, turmeric and paprika. Add lemon juice and oil, then leave to rest for over 1 hour.

Soak the coconut in the warm water. Cut the tomatoes into wedges.

Heat the ghee and cooking oil in a large saucepan. Fry the onions until brown. Add the garlic, ginger and salt, then stir for 2 minutes. Stir in the fresh coconut with its water. Add the limri, chilli powder, turmeric, green chillies, soomph, sugar and 2 tbsp of the dhania leaves. Cook, covered, for 15 minutes.

Open, then stir in the tomato paste. Cook carefully for a further 15 minutes to reduce the sauce to a thicker consistency. (Cook the sauce until the oil rises to the surface in small bubbles. This indicates that the sauce is ready.) If more gravy is required, add more warm water at this stage. Stir in the cream.

Gently add the seafood, cover, and leave to simmer for another 15 minutes. Garnish with the remaining dhania leaves, and serve with rice, salad and a tomato relish or yoghurt.

**Time: 1 hour**
**Serves 6**

Goan seafood curry

# Rice & Pulses

*Rice may be enriched with kesar (saffron), nuts and sultanas to produce the tantalising fragrance and flavour of a pilau. It may also be served plain with lentils and vegetables.*

*Whichever way it is prepared, rice remains the staple food of millions in Asia. For the vegetarians of southern and eastern India, rice is the heart of every meal, with a huge mound of white rice always at the centre of the thali or platter. Breakfast in the south includes delicious dosa and idli, rice cakes served with a lentil gravy.*

*There are at least 26 different kinds of rice, but the most popular for savoury cooking are the long-grained patnas. Basmati, with its natural nutty flavour, is considered the best, and as with so many good things, its flavour improves with age.*

*Rice has a wider significance in India. Grains of rice symbolising prosperity, wealth and fertility are sprinkled during holy ceremonies. It is considered an act of worship to fill the bowl of a wandering sadhu or holy man with cooked rice. Hindu priests are often presented with a bag of rice after a religious ceremony, as a sign of thanksgiving.*

# How to cook rice

It is surprising how many competent cooks find producing a pot of perfect rice a difficult task. Yet rice is one of the easiest foods to prepare if you keep a few basic rules in mind.

For six people, you need 500 g rice. If you are using basmati rice, first spread it on a tray and pick it over to remove husks and stones, then soak it in plenty of water. Leave the rice to stand for 30 minutes. Soaking rice removes the starchy powder that coats the grains, thus preventing them from sticking together or disintegrating during cooking. The rice also absorbs some of the water, which reduces the cooking period by half.

Bring 1 litre (4 cups) water to boil in a saucepan. Rinse the soaked rice several times in cold water to rid it of starch. The rice is ready to be cooked when the rinsing water is clear. Stir 5 ml (1 tsp) salt into the boiling water before gently dropping in the rice. Stir, then bring the pot to a rapid boil again. You may add 5 ml (1 tsp) butter or oil to prevent the starchy water from overflowing. Cover the saucepan and boil the rice for 10 to 15 minutes, when it should still be undercooked and firm.

Remove the saucepan from the heat, pour the rice into a suitable colander and allow cold water to run through, to remove any remaining starch. (In India, this starch water is sometimes saved for use in other cooking.)

At this stage there are two ways to complete the cooking of the rice. Return the starch-free rice to the saucepan. Add 15 ml (3 tsp) ghee or butter, then simmer over a low heat for 20 minutes. Use a fork to stir and separate the grains. Alternatively, steam the rice in a stainless steel colander, over 500 ml (2 cups) boiling water. Place the colander in the saucepan, cover with a lid, and simmer for 15 to 20 minutes until the rice is soft. Use a fork to fluff up the grains.

# Biryani

The royal dish of Indian cuisine is undoubtedly the Moghul biryani. This delicately spiced, basmati rice dish, with its subtle hint of kesar (saffron), was the food of maharajas and maharanis.

A biryani is prepared with a base of chicken, lamb, fish, prawns or vegetables, marinated in buttermilk until tender. Fried onions, lentils and golden-coated potatoes are layered in an ovenproof dish, traditionally sealed securely with dough to lock in the kesar and spice aroma.

It is served with spiced dahi, a cold buttermilk drink that is poured over as a gravy or served in small glasses as a drink. Biryani is best served on a large platter or silver tray. I usually decorate it with halved hard-boiled eggs and strips of the pure silver, edible paper used in India for festive dishes. For an exotic touch, surround the biryani with fresh hibiscus or frangipani flowers. Biryani is eaten with a special cucumber salad and other fresh kachoomers (salads). It may be made a day ahead and reheated in a slow oven for 30 minutes. First sprinkle with 125 ml (½ cup) water.

Ramola and Pradeep Parbhoo in the ancient city of Varanasi (Benaras), descending the steps of the ghats to touch the sacred River Ganges

# CHICKEN BIRYANI | *MURGHI BIRYANI*

1 large (1.5 kg) chicken, cut into pieces
3 ml (½ tsp) kesar (saffron)
200 ml (¾ cup) warm water
1 kg white or basmati rice
salt for rice
375 ml (1½ cups) melted ghee or
ghee and oil blend
500 ml (2 cups) brown lentils
3 onions, sliced
6 potatoes, halved
4 tuj (cinnamon sticks), 5 cm each
6 elachi (cardamom pods)
6 hard-boiled eggs, peeled
25 ml (½ cup) dhania (coriander)
leaves, chopped

### MARINADE
60 ml (¼ cup) dhania (coriander)
leaves, chopped
5 ml (1 tsp) turmeric
8 ml (1½ tsp) salt
10 ml (2 tsp) green masala
8 ml (1½ tsp) fresh ginger, pounded
5 ml (1 tsp) fresh garlic, pounded
2 green chillies, sliced lengthwise
250 ml (1 cup) sour milk or buttermilk

Wash the chicken and pat dry. Combine the marinade ingredients. Pour over the chicken and leave for 3 to 5 hours.

Place the kesar in a small saucepan with the water. Bring to the boil, simmer for 10 minutes, then set aside. I use this method to draw as much colour and flavour from the kesar as possible.

Wash the rice and bring to the boil in plenty of salted water. Parboil until it is soft yet firm to the touch. Place the rice in a colander and run cold water through to drain off any excess starch. Season the rice with an additional 1 t salt and mix in ½ cup of the melted ghee.

Wash the lentils, then boil them in unsalted water for about 20 minutes or until soft. Drain off excess water.

While the lentils are cooking, pour the remaining 1 cup ghee in a large pan. Fry the onions until golden, then remove from the pan. In the same pan, fry the uncooked potatoes to a light golden-brown colour, so that they are crispy (use more ghee if necessary.)

In a large pot with a well-fitting lid, suitable for use in the oven, pour the leftover ghee from the frying. Add the tuj and elachi, then spread a third of the rice evenly over the bottom of the pot. Sprinkle a third of the lentils over the rice, then add the chicken, with the marinade spread evenly over it. Spread another third of the rice over the chicken, then add the onions as a layer, followed by the potatoes. Top with the remaining lentils. Arrange the eggs on top, then cover with the remaining rice.

Pour the kesar water evenly over the dish. The kesar will give the rice a light yellow colour. Finally, sprinkle the dhania leaves over the top. To lock in the aroma, seal the pot with a sheet of foil. Cover with the lid and leave undisturbed for 90 minutes in an oven preheated to 170°C.

Serve with spiced dahi (buttermilk).

### TO FREEZE
Biryani freezes very well for about 2 months, but if doing so, omit the potatoes and eggs.

**Time: 2½ hours, plus 3 to 5 hours marinating**
**Serves 6 to 8**

# EASY CHICKEN BIRYANI | EASY MURGHI BIRYANI

*If you're in a hurry and don't have an hour to spend in preparation, try this quicker chicken biryani method.*

2 kg skinless chicken pieces
1 kg long-grain white rice
250 ml (1 cup) brown lentils
4 onions, finely sliced
250 ml (1 cup) ghee or cooking oil
4 large potatoes, peeled and halved
250 ml (1 cup) yoghurt or buttermilk
2 tomatoes, chopped
4 bay leaves
5 ml (1 tsp) kesar (saffron)

### MARINADE
10 ml (2 tsp) salt
5 ml (1 tsp) turmeric (optional)
15 ml (1 tbsp) fresh ginger, pounded
15 ml (1 tbsp) fresh garlic, pounded
10 ml (2 tsp) red masala
10 ml (2 tsp) green masala
30 ml (2 tbsp) dhania (coriander)
leaves, chopped

Marinate the chicken overnight in the combined marinade ingredients, in the refrigerator. Boil the rice in salted water until soft to the touch. Rinse with cold water in a colander to remove extra starch. Set aside.

Boil the lentils until cooked. Drain any excess liquid, then set aside. Fry the onions in ½ C ghee, remove, then set aside. In the same pan, fry the potatoes in another ½ C ghee until brown. Remove and set aside.

Arrange the chicken pieces in a large pot, add the yoghurt and tomatoes, then cover and steam for about 30 minutes over a medium heat. Set aside.

Mix the rice and lentils in a large bowl.

Finally, place the potatoes in a large pot with any leftover ghee and add the bay leaves. Cover with half the quantity of rice, then layer the chicken over with the gravy. Cover with the remaining rice.

Soak the kesar in a little hot water for a few minutes, then pour over the rice. Cover the pot and steam gently for 1 hour or until the chicken is cooked and tender.

**Time: 2 hours**
**Serves 6**

# SPICY RICE CHICKEN | *MURGHI AKHANI*

1.5 kg chicken cut in pieces and skinned
3 tomatoes, grated
500 ml (2 cups) basmati or long-grain
white rice, well washed
5 ml (1 tsp) gharum masala
45 ml (3 tbsp) dhania (coriander)
leaves, chopped

### MARINADE
5 ml (1 tsp) fresh ginger, pounded
5 ml (I tsp) fresh garlic, pounded
15 ml (1 tbsp) salt
15 ml (1 tbsp) lemon juice
8 ml (1½ tsp) red masala
8 ml (1½ tsp) turmeric
15 ml (1 tbsp) cooking oil

### VAGAAR
60 ml (4 tbsp) cooking oil or ghee
6 lavang (whole cloves)
5 elachi (cardamom pods)
3 tuj (cinnamon sticks), 5 cm each
1½ onions, chopped
4 potatoes, halved
750 ml (3 cups) warm water

Wash the chicken and drain. Combine the marinade ingredients, then rub well over the chicken and leave to marinate for at least 1 hour.

For the vagaar, heat the oil in a large saucepan, add the lavang, elachi and tuj, and brown for 10 seconds. Mix in the onions and fry until golden brown. Add the chicken and braise for 10 minutes so that the spices coat the chicken. Stir in the potatoes and water, and cook, covered, for 10 minutes over a medium heat.

Add the tomatoes and rice. Stir well. Add 1 C water. Cover the pot and cook very slowly until the rice has cooked (about 15 minutes).

Sprinkle gharum masala over the chicken and garnish with the dhania leaves.

**Time: 1 hour, plus 1 hour marinating**
**Serves 6 to 8**

# ROYAL LAMB BIRYANI | *SHAHJAHANI GOSHT BIRYANI*

*This succulent lamb biryani may be garnished with cashew nuts, lightly fried in ghee.*

1.5 kg lamb (any cut)
3 ml (½ tsp) kesar (saffron)
200 ml (¾ cup) warm water
1 kg white or basmati rice, well washed
375 ml (1½ cups) melted ghee or ghee and oil blend
500 ml (2 cups) brown lentils, washed
3 onions, sliced
6 potatoes, halved
4 tuj (cinnamon sticks), 5 cm each
6 elachi (cardamom pods)
6 hard-boiled eggs, peeled

MARINADE
60 ml (¼ cup) dhania (coriander) leaves, chopped
5 ml (1 tsp) turmeric
8 ml (1½ tsp) salt
10 ml (2 tsp) green masala
10 ml (2 tsp) fresh ginger, pounded
5 ml (1 tsp) fresh garlic, pounded
2 green chillies, sliced lengthwise
500 ml (2 cups) sour milk or buttermilk

GARNISH
125 ml (½ cup) dhania (coriander) leaves, chopped
2 onions, sliced and fried in
60 ml (4 tbsp) ghee

Wash the lamb and pat dry. Combine the marinade ingredients and pour over the lamb. Marinate for 3 to 5 hours.

In a small saucepan, bring the kesar and warm water to the boil, then simmer for 10 minutes and set aside to draw maximum colour and flavour.

Parboil the rice in plenty of salted water, until soft yet firm to the touch. Place in a colander and run cold water through to remove any excess starch. Season the rice with an extra 1 t salt and mix in ½ cup of the melted ghee.

Boil the lentils in unsalted water for about 20 minutes, or until soft. Drain off any excess water.

While the lentils are cooking, place the remaining 1 cup ghee in a large pan with the 3 sliced onions and fry until golden brown. Remove from the pan and set aside. Fry the potatoes in the same pan to a golden-brown colour, until they are crispy (use more ghee if necessary).

Pour the ghee left over from frying into a large, ovenproof dish with a well-fitting lid. Add the tuj and elachi, then spread a third of the rice evenly over the bottom of the dish. Sprinkle over a third of the lentils, then layer the lamb with the marinade spread evenly over it, on top. Spread another third of the rice over the lamb. Next, sprinkle over the 3 fried onions, followed by the fried potatoes. Top with the remaining lentils, then the eggs and cover with the remaining rice. Pour the saffron water evenly over the dish, to give it a light yellow colour.

Finally, garnish with the dhania leaves and the 2 fried onions; they will keep the rice moist. Seal with foil to lock in the aroma, cover the pot and cook undisturbed for 2 hours in an oven preheated to 170°C.

Serve with spiced dahi (buttermilk).

**Time: 2½ hours, plus 3 to 5 hours marinating**
**Serves 6 to 8**

# VEGETABLE BIRYANI | *BHAJI BIRYANI*

1 kg long-grain white or basmati rice
5 lavang (whole cloves)
3 tuj (cinnamon sticks), 5 cm each
5 elachi (cardamom pods)
500 g (2 cups) brown lentils
2 large onions, sliced
375 ml (1½ cups) ghee or oil
6 potatoes, halved
1 kg frozen mixed vegetables
200 g cabbage, washed and halved
200 g mushrooms, quartered (optional)
5 ml (1 tsp) turmeric
8 ml (1½ tsp) salt
10 ml (2 tsp) green masala
15 ml (1 tbsp) sugar
5 ml (1 tsp) fresh ginger, pounded
5 ml (1 tsp) fresh garlic, pounded
2 chillies, sliced lengthwise
10 limri (curry leaves)
125 ml (½ cup) dhania (coriander) leaves, chopped
375 ml (1½ cup) buttermilk
3 ml (½ tsp) kesar (saffron), soaked for 15 minutes in 125 ml (½ cup) hot water

Parboil the rice in salted water with the lavang, tuj and elachi. Drain in a colander and run cold water through to remove excess starch.

Wash the lentils and cook in 2 cups unsalted water for 30 minutes until soft. Fry the onions in ½ cup ghee until golden brown. Remove the onions and fry the potatoes until golden brown in the remaining ghee (add more if needed).

In a large bowl, mix together the frozen vegetables, cabbage, mushrooms, turmeric, salt, masala, sugar, ginger, garlic, chillies, limri and half the dhania leaves. Pour the buttermilk over.

Pour ½ cup ghee into a large, ovenproof dish. Layer a third of the rice, then a third of the lentils, then spread the vegetables evenly. Follow this with the second third of the rice, then the onions and potatoes.

Cover with the remaining lentils and rice. Pour the saffron water and ¼ cup ghee over the top. Sprinkle with 1 t salt and the remaining dhania leaves.

Bake in a preheated oven at 180°C for 1 hour.

**Time: 1½ hours**
**Serves 6 to 8**

# FISH BIRYANI | *MACHI BIRYANI*

*The aroma of kesar (saffron) permeates an exquisite rice dish laden with fish,*
*onions, spices and herbs. Use fresh kingklip, or prawns for a more elaborate occasion.*

500 g filleted fresh fish
625 ml (2½ cups) white rice
125 ml (½ cup) cooking oil
125 ml (½ cup) melted ghee or cooking oil
3 onions, sliced
5 ml (1 tsp) fresh garlic, pounded
5 ml (1 tsp) green masala
10 ml (2 tsp) dhania (coriander) seeds, coarsely crushed
10 ml (2 tsp) large soomph (aniseed), finely crushed
3 ml (½ tsp) salt
2 tomatoes, grated
125 ml (½ cup) buttermilk
60 ml (4 tbsp) dhania (coriander) leaves, chopped
3 ml (½ tsp) kesar (saffron), soaked in
125 ml (½ cup) boiled water then cooled

MARINADE
15 ml (1 tbsp) cooking oil
5 ml (1 tsp) salt
3 ml (½ tsp) turmeric
3 ml (½ tsp) chilli powder

Cut the fish into pieces, about 8 x 8 cm. Wash them and pat dry. Mix the marinade ingredients into a paste and rub over the fish. Marinate for 2 hours.

Parboil the rice in salted water. While still slightly undercooked, drain in a colander. Run cold water through to remove excess starch.

Fry the marinated fish in oil until light brown on both sides. Set aside.

Heat the ghee in a saucepan and fry the onions until soft. Remove half the onions and set aside. Add the garlic, masala, dhania seeds, soomph, salt and tomatoes to the onions in the pot. Cover and cook for 10 minutes. Add the fried fish, then cover with the buttermilk and half the dhania leaves.

Preheat the oven to 180°C. Place half the rice in an ovenproof dish or pot. Spread the fish with its gravy over the rice. Cover with the remaining rice. Pour the kesar mixture over. Garnish with the remaining dhania leaves, cover with a lid or foil and bake in the oven for 40 minutes.

**Time: 1 hour, plus 2 hours marinating**
**Serves 6**

Fish biryani and vegetable biryani,
served with spiced buttermilk and papadums

# YELLOW LENTIL RICE | *KHITCHERI*

*According to Indian folklore, a sure way of indicating to house guests that you are tiring of their visits is to offer them plain khudi and khitcheri. Khitcheri is a delicate rice dish topped with the hot sour-milk gravy known as khudi. If, however, it is served with fried fish, a spinach curry and crunchy onion salad, it would make your guests stay even longer!*

500 ml (2 cups) white rice
250 ml (1 cup) oil lentils (toover dhal)
750 ml (3 cup) boiling water
5 ml (1 tsp) salt
3 ml (½ tsp) turmeric
45 ml (3 tbsp) butter

Wash and soak the rice for 15 minutes. Pick over, then soak the lentils for 30 minutes.

In a saucepan, mix together the rice, lentils, boiling water, salt, turmeric and butter. Cover and bring to the boil, then reduce the heat and cook gently for 40 minutes until the rice is tender. Stir with a knife to separate the grains. (To avoid burning the rice, the pot may be placed on a toaster grill or aluminium pad while cooking.) Serve hot with the khudi (see below).

**Time: 1½ hours**
**Serves 4 to 6**

# HOT BUTTERMILK GRAVY | *KHUDI*

*Khudi is the smooth and thick yellow buttermilk gravy that accompanies the mound of piping hot yellow rice called khitcheri. Limri (curry leaves) and garlic complement the buttermilk superbly.*

500 ml (2 cup) buttermilk
125 ml (½ cup) water
30 ml (2 tbsp) chana flour
5 ml (1 tsp) green masala
3 ml (½ tsp) turmeric
3 ml (½ tsp) fresh garlic, pounded
15 ml (1 tbsp) dhania (coriander) leaves, chopped
3 ml (½ tsp) salt
10 curry leaves (fresh or dried)

VAGAAR
30 ml (2 tbsp) ghee or cooking oil
5 ml (1 tsp) jeero (cumin seeds)
5 ml (1 tsp) rai (mustard seeds)
8 limri (curry leaves)

In a bowl, beat the non-vagaar ingredients for 2 minutes with an eggbeater.

To make the vagaar, heat the ghee in a pot, then brown the spices until brown for 10 to 12 seconds. Quickly pour the buttermilk mixture into the pot and leave on a high heat. Stir until it boils, then remove from the heat. (It is imperative to keep stirring or the buttermilk will curdle.)

Spoon a small amount of khudi over each helping of khitcheri. Khudi may also be served in small bowls, to be poured over the khitcheri or drunk.

**Time: 20 minutes**
**Serves 4 to 6**

# EGG-FRIED RICE | *INDA PILAU*

*This is a delicious egg and rice combination that makes for an easy supper dish. Serve it with garlic-chilli sauce.*

375 ml (1½ cups) basmati or long-grain rice
125 ml (½ cup) cooking oil
3 eggs, beaten
2 onions, sliced
1 green chilli, finely chopped
5 ml (1 tsp) fresh garlic, pounded
3 ml (½ tsp) salt
125 ml (½ cup) dhania (coriander) leaves, chopped

Wash the rice several times and boil in salted water for 10 to 15 minutes until soft. Drain any excess water.

Heat the oil in a large pan, then stir in the egg until cooked. Add the onions, chilli and garlic, and fry for 2 to 3 minutes. Add the rice, sprinkle with salt and mix well. Fry for 5 minutes, tossing the rice continually. Garnish with the chopped dhania leaves.

**Time: 45 minutes**
**Serves 6**

# AROMATIC RICE | *VAGAARELI CHAVAL*

*This delicate dish enhances the nutty flavour of basmati rice. I serve it with roasts and dry meat dishes.*

625 ml (2½ cups) long-grain or basmati rice
5 ml (1 tsp) salt
125 ml (½ cup) water

VAGAAR
45 ml (3 tbsp) ghee or cooking oil
5 elachi (cardamom pods)
5 lavang (whole cloves)
3 tuj (cinnamon sticks), 4 cm each
2 large onions, chopped

Boil the rice in salted water, then rinse out excess starch in a colander with cold water. Season with more salt if desired.

To make the vagaar, heat the ghee (use more if necessary) in a large flat saucepan with a lid. Add the elachi, lavang and tuj, then stir in the onions and brown over a medium heat for 3 to 5 minutes.

Mix the rice into the onion mixture. Add the water and simmer, covered, on the lowest heat for 30 minutes or until the rice has heated through and absorbed the aromas.
**Time: 1 hour**
**Serves 4 to 6**

VARIATION
Clean and soak ½ cup chana lentils in 2 cups boiling water for 30 minutes. Drain and precook with the rice, adding 1 t jeero (cumin seeds).

Follow the recipe above.

A vegetarian treat: hot buttermilk gravy, yellow lentil rice and potato fry, accompanied by sambals, sliced onions, vegetable pickle and mango chundoo

# Pulses

The Orientals realised the wisdom of using moong sprouts centuries ago. Elsewhere, these crisp delicacies were only discovered in recent times and their high nutritional value acknowledged. Moong sprouts are today the major source of protein sold at health stores for vegetarians. Their popularity and demand has spread to supermarkets as well.

Moong lentils, like fenugreek seeds, wheat and dried beans, are easily sprouted at home. Sprouting softens the hard lentils and expands the storehouse of vitamins and minerals. Wheat, for instance, yields 600 per cent more vitamin C when sprouted, and moong sprouts contain enough protein to be classed as a total food, with a very high mineral and multi-vitamin content.

Moong sprouts are extremely versatile. Use them in salads and soups or as a main vegetarian dish. My own children love the crunchy addition of raw moong sprouts over their potato salad. (I usually also add some soya sauce for additional Oriental flavour.)

## How to sprout lentils or beans

My grandmother's village method of sprouting lentils is the simplest I have encountered. My mother passed this basic Indian method on to me.

Sort and pick over the lentils, then rinse them several times. Place in a deep bowl, cover with plenty of boiling water and leave to soak for 12 hours (during which time the lentils will expand). Pour off the excess water and spread the lentils out on a soft kitchen cloth or muslin. Roll up the cloth into the shape of a sausage and place in a dish.

Leave undisturbed at room temperature for 1 to 2 days, until the lentils have sprouted (it takes longer in cold weather). When the sprouts have grown about 12 mm long, place them in the refrigerator. They are now ready for use.

Sprouts may be frozen for about 2 months.

## Identifying Beans, peas & Lentils

### Black-eyed beans
LOMBHIA BEANS
These beige, oval-shaped beans have a slightly smokey flavour and are prepared in the same manner as whole moong.

### Dried Indian beans
CHORI BEANS
These dark brown beans are round and flat with a spot on one side. They provide a sumptuous main dish for vegetarians.

### Red kidney beans
RAIMA BEANS

These dark red, kidney-shaped beans are a particular favourite in Bengal and the Punjab. They may be prepared in the same manner as whole moong.

Raima beans are especially delicious when prepared with lamb or mutton. I often boil them with onions, a few cinnamon sticks and salt, and serve them with a generous blob of butter. My children love this dish on a cold winter's night.

### Split Indian beans
VAAL NI DHAL

These large, creamy-coloured beans have a rather powdery texture and a slightly bitter flavour. They are prepared in the same manner as split moong.

### Whole green moong (mung beans)
MUGH

These dark green, oval lentils have a mild aromatic flavour, which is enhanced by the introduction of a pinch of asafoetida (hing) during cooking.

Under the label 'mung bean', moong has received worldwide acclaim as a health food. When sprouted it is highly nutritious, especially when eaten raw. Moong is the most popular north Indian dhal.

### Other beans

A variety of the more common beans, such as kidney beans, haricot and lady beans, are also used in Indian cookery.

### Split chickpeas
CHANA DHAL

These lentils are second only to wheat in nutritional value. In their whole form they are known as chickpeas. Ghana is the split form, resembling yellow corn in shape and colour. They also resemble the yellowish split peas sold in supermarkets.

Ghana dhal is ground into chana flour, the only flour used for traditional Indian savouries such as chilli bites or the deep-fried noodles called sev.

Ghana dhal acts as a general health tonic when it is steeped in water overnight and chewed in the morning with a helping of honey.

### Whole chickpeas
WHOLE CHANA

These large, heart-shaped, beige peas are India's favourite snack food, whether spiced, boiled, grilled or crushed. With their high nutritional value, chana may definitely not be dismissed as junk food.

Kabuli chana is a variety that is prepared as a delicious dish garnished with onion rings and served with large puri or fried breads.

## Black gram
### URAD DHAL

These small, round, off-white lentils are distinguished by their black husks. They are usually prepared in combination with oil dhal, chana and the split moong dhal. Urad dhal are used in idli, the southern Indian breakfast cakes, as a kind of leaven.

Urad dhal is extremely popular in northern India. Shelled and cooked in milk, the lentils are thought to promote vigour and to increase the breastmilk of feeding mothers.

Strange as it may sound, a small quantity of the whole urad dhal is placed in a hookah (an Indian smoking pipe) and smoked as a cure for hiccups.

## Brown lentils
### MASOOR DHAL

These round, flat lentils are used specifically for biryanis or rice dishes, and may also be made into a soup. Their earthy flavour can be dull unless well spiced–I use curry leaves and fresh chillies to improve the flavour of these lentils.

## Oil lentils
### TOOVER (TUR) DHAL

The dried, split form of toover beans, which grow in pods, these round, flat, dark yellow lentils have
a natural oil content–hence the name oil lentil.

Toover are the most commonly used lentils, eaten almost daily in most parts of India as a thick soup poured over a mound of rice. They have a pleasing flavour and may be used for sweet dishes as well.

Since they are usually cooked into a smooth soup, toover are hardly recognisable as lentils when served.

## Pink split lentils
### MASOOR NI DHAL

These round, flat salmon-coloured lentils are actually brown lentils in split form, with the outer husks removed.

Quick to cook, with a pleasant, mild taste, they easily absorb the flavour of curry leaves, whole green chillies and garlic. They can be prepared into delicious soup in a very short period. (The pink shade turns dull yellow, so do not be surprised.)

## Yellow split moong lentils
### MOONG DHAL (MUGH NI DHAL)

These small, yellow, oval-shaped and flat lentils are the split form of whole moong, with a markedly different taste. They are often prepared as a side dish for vegetarian meals. Moong dhal should maintain their shape when cooked, like separate grains of rice.

As a variation, moong dhal may also be made into a thick dhal or soup that is eaten with warm roti.

Toover dhal

Chori beans

Masoor

Vaal ni dhal

Masoor ni dhal

Split peas

Kidney beans

Lombhia beans

Chana dhal

Whole chana

Rajma beans

Papdi

White-speckled
sugar beans

Haricot beans

Moong dhal

Moong

Urad dhal

# THICK OIL LENTILS | *TOOVER DHAL*

*This dhal is always served over a helping of rice, with spiced vegetable dishes such as green peas,
green beans or brinjals. Together with rice, it forms the staple diet in India. Dhal may also be served
as a thick soup with hot toast in winter. Mango pickle and papadums are a traditional accompaniment.*

250 ml (1 cup) oil lentils
750 ml (3 cups) warm water
1 medium onion, chopped
2 gem squashes, peeled and cubed
or 100 g pumpkin, cubed (add a piece of
pineapple for flavour if you like)
15 ml (1 tbsp) oil or ghee
5 ml (1 tsp) red masala
5 ml (1 tsp) fresh ginger, pounded
5 ml (1 tsp) turmeric
5 ml (1 tsp) salt
8 ml (1½ tsp) sugar
10 ml (2 tsp) lemon juice
15 ml (1 tbsp) ghee or cooking oil
3 ml (½ tsp) methi (fenugreek) seeds
8 limri (curry leaves)
2 tomatoes, grated

VAGAAR

30 ml (2 tbsp) cooking oil or ghee
1 whole dried red chilli
3 ml (½ tsp) methi (fenugreek) seeds
3 ml (½ tsp) ground hing (asafoetida)

GARNISH

15 ml (1 tbsp) dhania (coriander)
leaves, chopped

Pick over the lentils and soak them in 2 cups hot water for 30
minutes. Rinse the lentils several times and place in a pot with
the warm water, onion, squashes and oil. Cover and simmer
for about 40 minutes over a medium heat until it thickens to a
soup-like consistency. Add the remaining ingredients to the pot
and whisk well with an eggbeater until smooth.

To make the vagaar, heat the oil in a small pot, then brown the
chilli before adding the other spices. Quickly pour the vagaar
over the lentils, cover with a lid and simmer for 15 minutes.

Garnish with the dhania.

**Time: 45 minutes**
**Serves 6**

TIPS

If you want to precook the lentils, they may be cooked in a
pressure cooker. After cooking, you may also freeze half the
quantity for later use. When required, add the masalas and
make a fresh vagaar.

# RED LENTILS & SPINACH | *BHAJI MASOOR NI DHAL*

625 ml (2½ cups) red lentils
1 litre (4 cup) water
1 medium onion, chopped
200 g spinach, shredded
5 ml (1 tsp) salt
3 ml (½ tsp) fresh garlic, pounded
2 green chillies, sliced lengthwise
3 ml (½ tsp) turmeric
6 limri (curry leaves)
45 ml (3 tbsp) cooking oil
3 ml (½ tsp) rai (mustard seeds)

Wash the lentils well. In a saucepan, bring the water to the boil, then add the lentils, onion, spinach, salt, garlic, chillies, turmeric, limri and ½ tbsp of the oil. Cover the saucepan and simmer for 30 minutes.

Heat the remaining oil in a small saucepan. Fry the rai and when they stop spluttering, add the mixture to the lentil pot. Stir, then simmer for 10 minutes.

Serve hot with steamed rice.

**Time: 45 minutes**
**Serves 6 to 8**

# GREEN MOONG LENTILS | *MUGH*

*After a heavy Sunday meal, simple yet satisfying mugh is perfect for Monday. Eat it with hot roti, onion salad and spicy fried fish.*

375 ml (1½ cups) moong lentils
750 ml (3 cups) boiling water
1 large onion, chopped
5 ml (1 tsp) red masala
3 ml (½ tsp) fresh ginger, pounded
5 ml (1 tsp) salt
3 ml (½ tsp) turmeric
1 large ripe tomato, grated
5 ml (1 tsp) lemon juice

### VAGAAR
45 ml (3 tbsp) cooking oil
1 dried red chilli
2 ml (½ tsp) ground hing (asafoetida)
or 5 ml (1 tsp) jeero (cumin seeds)

### GARNISH
30 ml (2 tbsp) dhania (coriander) leaves, chopped

Pick over the lentils, wash several times and soak in water for 20 minutes, then drain. Place the lentils in a deep saucepan with the boiling water. Cover, then boil rapidly for 15 minutes.

Add the onion, cover again and cook over a medium heat for approximately 20 minutes, or until the lentils are soft. Stir to prevent sticking. Mix in the masala, ginger, salt, turmeric, tomato and lemon juice. Allow the moong to reduce to a thick gravy.

Whisk the moong with an eggbeater into a semi-smooth consistency.

To make the vagaar, heat the oil in a large saucepan, then add the chilli and ground hing. Finally, mix in the moong mixture, cover, reduce the heat and simmer for 10 to 15 minutes.

Garnish with dhania leaves.

**Time: 1 hour, plus 20 minutes soaking**
**Serves 6**

# HARICOT BEAN CURRY | *SOOKHI PAPDI NU SAKH*

*This is the standard recipe for any dried Indian beans, such as black-eyed, kidney or sugar beans. Haricot bean curry may be served with roti or puri. For a snack, try it on squares of toast. Always serve a sweet fruit pickle or a fresh relish, and papadums, with the bean curry.*

500 ml (2 cups) haricot beans, soaked overnight in hot water and drained
2 medium onions, chopped
1.5 litres (6 cups) boiling water
1 tomato, grated
30 ml (2 tbsp) dhania (coriander) leaves, chopped
10 ml (2 tsp) turmeric
5 ml (1 tsp) red masala
3 ml (½ tsp) fresh ginger, pounded
3 ml (½ tsp) fresh garlic, pounded
15 ml (3 tsp) dhania-jeero (coriander-cumin)
5 ml (1 tsp) salt

VAGAAR
45 ml (3 tbsp) cooking oil
1 dried whole red chilli
3 ml (½ tsp) ground hing (asafoetida)

GARNISH
fresh dhania (coriander) leaves, chopped

In a deep pot, cook the beans, onions and boiling water for 1½ hours or until the beans are very soft. (Leave the lid ajar so that the froth from the beans doesn't boil over.) You may freeze the beans at this stage.

Remove the beans from the heat and mix in the tomato, dhania leaves, turmeric, masala, ginger, garlic, dhania-jeero and salt.

For the vagaar, heat the oil in a pot, then add the chilli and brown for a few seconds. Sprinkle in the ground hing, add the bean mixture, cover immediately and simmer for 20 minutes over a medium heat. Stir frequently.

Garnish with dhania leaves.

**Time: 2 hours, plus overnight soaking**
**Serves 4**

# SPLIT CHICKPEA LENTILS | *CHANA DHAL*

*Chana dhal resembles sweetcorn and is cooked in a gravy thickened with gem squash,*
*onions and tomatoes. It is served with puri and a sweet, dried fruit pickle.*

500 ml (2 cups) split chickpea lentils
1 litre water
1 large onion, chopped
flesh of 1 gem squash, cubed
or 125 ml (½ cup) chopped Indian
marrow
15 ml (1 tbsp) cooking oil
1 tomato, chopped
3 ml (½ tsp) red masala
3 ml (½ tsp) fresh ginger, pounded
3 ml (½ tsp) fresh garlic, pounded
8 ml (1½ tsp) salt
5 ml (1 tsp) lemon juice
5 ml (1 tsp) turmeric
10 ml (2 tsp) dhania-jeero
(coriander-cumin)

VAGAAR
45 ml (3 tbsp) cooking oil
5 ml (1 tsp) jeero (cumin seeds)
or 2 tuj (cinnamon sticks), 5 cm each

GARNISH
dhania (coriander) leaves, chopped

Pick over the lentils, wash well and soak in plenty of warm water for about 30 minutes.

In a covered saucepan, bring the water to the boil, then add the lentils, squash, onion and oil. Simmer, covered, for 45 minutes until the lentils are soft but retain their shape. Stir in the tomato and seasonings.

For the vagaar, heat the oil, then brown the jeero or tuj. Add the lentil mixture, reduce the heat and simmer for 20 minutes.

Garnish with dhania leaves.

**Time: 1 hour, plus 30 minutes soaking**
**Serves 4 to 6**

TIP
If you find it difficult to peel the gem squash, boil it with the lentils, then scoop out the flesh (without the seeds) and mix well.

# MOONG SPROUTS | *VAVRA MUGH*

*Use sprouted moong lentils for this Gujerati or northern Indian dish, which is a vegetarian delicacy. Served with warm puri and an onion salad, it becomes a gourmet treat. The moong require 2 days to sprout to the required length.*

250 ml (1 cup) moong sprouts, 5 mm long
1 large onion, chopped
5 ml (1 tsp) salt
3 ml (½ tsp) turmeric
5 ml (1 tsp) green masala
3 ml (½ tsp) fresh ginger, pounded
3 ml (½ tsp) fresh garlic, pounded
10 ml (2 tsp) dhania-jeero (coriander-cumin)
250 ml (1 cup) warm water

VAGAAB
125 ml (½ cup) cooking oil
1 dried red chilli
5 ml (1 tsp) jeero (cumin seeds)
GARNISH
15 ml (1 tbsp) dhania (coriander) leaves, chopped

In a large bowl, mix together the moong sprouts, the onion, salt, turmeric, green masala, ginger, garlic and dhania-jeero.

To make the vagaar, heat the oil in a flat saucepan with a well-fitting lid. Brown the chilli, followed by the jeero seeds. Add the sprout mixture to the saucepan with the warm water. Cover the pot and cook over a medium heat for about 45 minutes. (The sprouts should be soft but not stick together.)

Garnish with the dhania leaves.

**Time: 1 hour, 1 to 2 days for sprouting**
**Serves 4**

Moong sprouts, green mung lentils and easy green bean curry (page 100) served with puri

# SPROUTED YELLOW SPLIT MOONG LENTILS |
## *VAVRA MUGH NI DHAL*

*The golden-yellow split moong lentils cook into loose grains, resembling yellow rice but with a softer texture.*
*This dish is ideally served with puri or roti, sweet, dried fruit pickles and onion salad.*

250 ml (1 cup) yellow split moong lentils
1 onion, chopped
3 ml (½ tsp) turmeric
3 ml (½ tsp) green masala
3 ml (½ tsp) salt
10 ml (2 tsp) dhania-jeero
(coriander-cumin)
375 ml (1½ cups) hot water

VAGAAR
60 ml (4 tbsp) ghee or cooking oil
5 ml (1 tsp) jeero (cumin seeds)
5 ml (1 tsp) fresh ginger, pounded

GARNISH
15 ml (1 tbsp) dhania (coriander)
leaves, chopped

Pick over the lentils, wash and soak in water for 30 minutes, then drain. Mix the lentils with the onion and spices.

For the vagaar, heat the ghee in a saucepan. Add the jeero and ginger, cover and brown for 10 seconds.

Add the moong mixture and hot water. Cover, then simmer gently over a low heat for 30 minutes. Stir with a fork to separate the grains.

Garnish with dhania leaves.

**Time: 40 minutes, plus 30 minutes soaking**
**Serves 4**

# YELLOW SPLIT MOONG LENTIL GRAVY | *MUGH NI DHAL ASCHEE*

250 ml (1 cup) yellow split moong lentils
1 tomato, chopped
1 onion, finely chopped
3 ml (½ tsp) green masala
3 ml (½ tsp) salt
2 ml (¼ tsp) turmeric
5 ml (1 tsp) garlic, pounded
5 ml (1 tsp) gharum masala
30 ml (2 tbsp) fresh dhania
(coriander) leaves

VAGAAR
30 ml (2 tbsp) ghee
1 dry red chill
3 ml (½ tsp) ground hing (asafoetida)

Pick over and wash the lentils. Cook them with the tomatoes until smooth. Set aside.

Heat the ghee in a pot, then fry the vagaar spices and onion until golden brown. Stir in the lentil mixture, the green masala, salt, turmeric and garlic, then simmer, covered, for 10 minutes.

Garnish with gharum masala and dhania leaves.

Serve with roti.

**Time: 45 minutes**
**Serves 4**

# MIXED LENTILS | *URAD TOOVER NI DHAL*

310 ml (1¼ cups) black gram
125 ml (½ cup) split chickpeas
125 ml (½ cup) oil lentils
5 ml (1 tsp) turmeric
5 ml (1 tsp) red masala
5 ml (1 tsp) salt
500 ml (2 cups) water

VAGAAR
45 ml (3 tbsp) ghee
3 ml (½ tsp) fresh ginger, pounded
5 ml (1 tsp) fresh garlic, pounded

GARNISH
5 ml (1 tsp) gharum masala
30 ml (2 tbsp) fresh dhania
(coriander) leaves

Pick over and soak the pulses in very hot water for 1 to 2 hours. Drain and wash well. Cook them with the spices, water and a drop of oil (to avoid boiling over), until very soft and sticky.

Heat the vagaar ingredients in another pot, then add the lentil mixture. Cook slowly for another 30 minutes. Garnish with gharum masala and dhania.

**Time: 1 hour**
**Serves 6**

# HOT CHICKPEA SPECIAL | *KABULI CHANA*

*In this special Eastern delicacy, chickpeas are cooked in a thick but delicately flavoured sweet-and-sour gravy.*
*It should be accompanied by Indian bread and a bowl of thinly sliced onions dressed with salt and lemon juice.*
*Alternatively, use the onion slices as a garnish.*

1½ litres (6 cups) hot water
625 ml (2½ cups) whole chickpeas,
soaked
overnight in plenty of water
45 ml (3 tbsp) cooking oil
15 ml (1 tbsp) chana flour
2 onions, chopped
8 ml (1½ tsp) red masala
1 to 2 green chillies, sliced lengthwise
20 ml (4 tsp) jeero (cumin seeds), dry
roasted and crushed
3 ml (½ tsp) turmeric
8 ml (1½ tsp) salt
3 potatoes, diced

60 g tamarind, soaked in 125 ml (½ cup)
water and strained (use purée)
30 ml (2 tbsp) ghor (sugar jaggery)
or 30 ml (2 tbsp) sugar or golden syrup
250 ml (1 cup) water

GARNISH
5 ml (1 tsp) gharum masala
a handful dhania (coriander) leaves,
chopped
lemon wedges

Bring the water to the boil, add the drained chickpeas and simmer for 1½ hours or until soft.

Heat the oil in a saucepan, sprinkle in the flour and stir for a few seconds. Add the onions and brown for 3 minutes. Add the red masala, chillies, 2 tsp of the jeero, the turmeric and salt. Stir for 2 minutes. Mix in the chickpeas. Add the potatoes, tamarind purée, ghor and water. Cover and simmer for 30 minutes.

Garnish with the remaining jeero, gharum masala, chopped dhania leaves and lemon wedges. Serve with a large puri.
**Time: 2 hours, plus overnight soaking**
**Serves 6**

# Vegetables

Because cabbages feature prominently on many vegetable stalls, I have found ways to use them to fullest advantage. For instance, I devised a Khubi Fry that is charming in its simplicity, yet is enhanced by the combination of onion and spices. This proves how one can experiment by using one's own preference for flavour.

The subtle flavour of this dish may seem out of character to those who expect Indian food to be hot or over-spiced but it illustrates the typical cooking of Gujerat in northern India, where the cook concentrates on retaining the individual character and texture of each main ingredient.

A platter of steamed vegetables of your choice can enhance any meal, provided they are as fresh as possible. Potato wedges, butternut chunks, baby marrow, green peppers (capsicum), garden peas, white cauliflower florettes, green string beans, baby carrots and broccoli are some of the vegetables that are best bought fresh at the markets.

Steam vegetables in very little water, without salt, over the gentlest of heat. Add 1 tsp jeero, then simmer until cooked yet firm. Dot with butter and season.

# GREEN PEAS IN THEIR PODS | *UMBARYO*

*In this dish, very young peas are cooked and eaten in their tender pods.*
*Serve it as a separate course or a most unusual starter.*

500 g young peas in their pods
1 potato, cut into thick chips
2 carrots
2 onions, halved
30 ml (2 tbsp) cooking oil
5 ml (1 tsp) ajowan seeds
2 ml (½ tsp) turmeric
5 ml (1 tsp) green masala
3 ml (½ tsp) salt

Thoroughly rinse the peas in their pods. Place all the ingredients in a heavy-based saucepan. Add enough water to cover, then boil gently for 20 to 30 minutes, until the pods are cooked but still firm.
**Time: 30 minutes**
**Serves 4 to 6**

# BRINJAL CURRY | *VENGAN CURRY*

*Brinjals (aubergine/eggplant) are bountiful and extremely versatile. This recipe could be used cooled as a filling*
*for sandwiches.*

500 g brinjals, washed and sliced
lengthwise
30 ml (2 tbsp) cooking oil
15 ml (1 tbsp) chana flour
30 ml (2 tbsp) water
5 ml (1 tsp) salt
3 ml (½ tsp) turmeric
5 ml (1 tsp) red masala
15 ml (1 tbsp) dhania-jeero
(coriander-cumin)
15 ml (1 tbsp) ghor (sugar jaggery) or
golden syrup
10 ml (2 tsp) brown sugar
3 tomatoes
10 ml (2 tbsp) dhania (coriander)
leaves, chopped

VAGAAR
75 ml (5 tbsp) cooking oil
5 ml (1 tsp) rai (mustard seeds)

Make criss-cross inserts over the white flesh of the brinjals, then rub in the oil.

Make a paste by mixing the flour and water. Add the salt, turmeric, masala, dhania-jeero, ghor and sugar, then mix well. Rub the paste over the brinjals.

For the vagaar, heat the oil in a large, flat saucepan. Add the spices and temper for a few seconds. Arrange the brinjals in the saucepan, side by side, then brown on both sides.

Grate the tomatoes and spread over the brinjals. Sprinkle dhania leaves over, cover and cook gently over a low to medium heat for about 45 minutes, or until the brinjals soften.
**Time: 1 hour**
**Serves 4 to 6**

VARIATION
In a saucepan, steam 2 brinjals in 1 cup water until soft. Remove and, when cool, peel. Mash the flesh with a fork, then season with ½ tsp salt. Heat 4 T oil in a pan, add 1 t pounded ginger and 1 tsp red masala, then brown. Add the brinjals and stir well. Serve with hot roti or on bread. It also makes a good dip or filling in a roll.

# SPINACH FRY | *BHAJI FRY*

*This makes an excellent side dish with fish curry and rice. It is also good on toast, as a snack.*

400 g (1 bunch) spinach
80 ml (1/3 cup) cooking oil
5 ml (1 tsp) jeero (cumin seeds)
2 onions, sliced
3 ml (½ tsp) fresh garlic, pounded
3 ml (½ tsp) red masala
3 ml (½ tsp) salt
2 ml (½ tsp) turmeric

Cut the thick veins from the spinach leaves. Soak the leaves in cold water for 5 minutes, rinse several times, then chop finely.

Heat the oil in a pan, add the jeero and brown for a few seconds. Add the onions and garlic, then fry until brown and soft. Mix in the spinach, red masala, salt and turmeric. Cook, uncovered, over a medium heat until all the moisture has evaporated from the spinach. Once the spinach has softened, stir, then serve.

**Time: 25 minutes**
**Serves 4**

# FRIED MADUMBI OR SPINACH LEAVES | *TARELA PATRA*

*Madumbis grow in tropical climates and the leaves (patra) resemble large elephant ears. Using spinach as an alternative is also delicious. Steam and serve as a light meal or as a snack with puffed puri and lemon wedges.*

250 ml (1 cup) chana flour
200 ml (½ cup) bread flour
200 ml (½ cup) maize flour
15 ml (1 tbsp) melted ghee
15 ml (1 tbsp) sugar
13 ml (2½ tsp) salt
3 ml (½ tsp) bicarbonate of soda
30 ml (2 tbsp) cooking oil
5 ml (1 tsp) green masala
5 ml (1 tsp) red masala
3 ml (½ tsp) fresh ginger, pounded
2 ml (½ tsp) ground hing (asafoetida)
3 ml (½ tsp) fresh garlic, pounded
5 ml (1 tsp) turmeric
10 ml (2 tsp) dhania-jeero
(coriander-cumin)
5 ml (1 tsp) gharum masala
5 ml (1 tsp) ajowan seeds
250 ml (1 cup) buttermilk
625 ml (2½ cups) water
25 small madumbi leaves or 1 large
bunch spinach
250 ml (1 cup) cooking oil for frying

Mix together all the ingredients other than the buttermilk, water, madumbi leaves and oil for frying. Stir in the buttermilk and water to create a soft batter, slightly thicker than a pancake batter.

Wash the madumbi or spinach leaves, cut off the stems and remove any thick veins so that the leaves may be flattened. Using a spatula, coat a leaf with about 1 tbsp batter. Cover with another leaf and spread again with another 1 tbsp batter. Prepare a pile of six leaves layered on top of each other, then fold the outer edges over and roll tightly into a swiss roll shape-approximately 10 cm in length. Place all the rolls into a steamer pot and cook for about 45 minutes.

Serve sliced with a drizzle of salad oil over the top or cut into rounds, shallow fry and serve over puris. The rolls may be frozen for later use.

**Time: 90 minutes**
**Serves 6**

# BRINJAL CURRY | *BATAKA NE VENGAN NU SAKH*

*Delicious on hot toast, or as an accompaniment to a meat dish.*

2 medium brinjals (aubergine/eggplant),
washed
4 large potatoes, cubed
2 medium onions, sliced
5 ml (1 tsp) salt
5 ml (1 tsp) red masala
3 ml (½ tsp) turmeric
10 ml (2 tsp) dhania-jeero
(coriander-cumin)

VAGAAR
45 ml (3 tbsp) cooking oil

3 ml (½ tsp) jeero (cumin seeds)
5 ml (1 tsp) ajowan seeds or 45 ml (3
tbsp) cooking oil
1 dried red chilli
5 ml (1 tsp) ground hing (asafoetida)
200 ml (½ cup) warm water

GARNISH
30 ml (2 tbsp) dhania (coriander) leaves,
chopped

Destem and dice the brinjals, but do not peel. In a large bowl, mix with the potatoes, onions, salt, masala, turmeric and dhania-jeero.

To make the vagaar, heat the oil in a pot and brown the spices quickly. Add the brinjal mixture. Pour in the water, cover and cook over a medium heat until the potatoes are cooked.

Garnish with coriander leaves.

**Time: 40 minutes**
**Serves 6**

Brinjal curry and green peas in their pods

# POTATO FRY | *BATAKA NI FRY*

*Potato fry may be served with toover dhal and rice, or with khitcheri and khudi. Children love this potato dish. Try it with sliced onions on hot toast as a snack, or use it as a sandwich filling.*

4 large potatoes, peeled and cubed
5 ml (1 tsp) green masala
3 ml (½ tsp) turmeric
10 ml (2 tsp) dhania-jeero
(coriander-cumin)
5 ml (1 tsp) salt
30 ml (2 tbsp) dhania (coriander)
leaves, chopped

VAGAAR
60 ml (4 tbsp) cooking oil
5 ml (1 tsp) rai (mustard seeds)
5 ml (1 tsp) jeero (cumin seeds)
3 ml (½ tsp) methi (fenugreek) seeds

Wash and mix the potatoes with the masala, turmeric, dhania-jeero, salt and half the dhania leaves.

To make the vagaar, heat the oil in a large, flat saucepan or frying pan, add the spices and brown for 10 seconds.

Add the potatoes, toss gently, then cover and simmer for 15 minutes. Remove the lid and fry the potatoes for 7 minutes until crispy. Garnish with the remaining dhania leaves.
**Time: 25 minutes**
**Serves 6**

# EASY GREEN BEAN CURRY | *PAPADI NU SAKH*

*This quick green bean recipe (also suitable for green peas, potatoes, aubergine/eggplant or okra) can be prepared to serve with roasts and salads.*

500 g green beans, fresh or frozen, cut
into 2.5 cm lengths
60 ml (4 tbsp) cooking oil
5 ml (1 tsp) ajowan seeds or jeero
(cumin seeds)
1 large onion, sliced
2 green chillies, finely chopped
5 ml (1 tsp) fresh garlic, pounded
10 ml (2 tsp) sugar
5 ml (1 tsp) salt
3 ml (½ tsp) turmeric

Wash and drain the beans. Heat the oil in heavy saucepan, then fry the ajowan seeds for 15 seconds. Add the beans and remaining ingredients to the saucepan, stir, cover and simmer for 20 minutes over a low heat. Remove the lid and cook, gently, for a further 15 minutes to reduce the moisture.
**Time: 30 minutes**
**Serves 4 to 6**

# SPICY GREEN BEANS | *PAPADI NE VENGAN NU SAKH*

*This side dish may also be made with fresh beans such as gwarferi, toover ni sing, papadi or toover sing, although frozen green beans may also be used. It will make a substantial meal served with warm roti or hot toast and pickles. You could even try it as a topping combined with crunchy sliced onions and cheese on a slice of wholewheat bread (placed under the grill for a few minutes). As a variation, add 100 g green peas.*

500 g green beans, cut into 4 cm lengths

VAGAAR
80 ml (⅓ cup) cooking oil
a blend of 1 dried red chilli and a pinch ground hing (asafoetida)
or 5 ml (1 tsp) jeero (cumin seeds)
5 ml (1 tsp) fresh ginger, pounded
1 small onion, chopped
5 ml (1 tsp) turmeric

3 ml (½ tsp) salt

3 ml (½ tsp) red masala
2 potatoes, cut into 4 cm cubes
100 g brinjals (aubergine/eggplant), skinned and cut into 2.5 cm cubes
5 ml (1 tsp) dhania-jeero (coriander-cumin)
1 tomato, finely chopped
15 ml (1 tbsp) dhania (coriander) leaves, chopped

Wash the green beans and drain in a colander.

For the vagaar, heat the oil in a saucepan. Add the chilli/hing blend (or the jeero), ginger and onions, then fry for 2 to 3 minutes until the onions are translucent.

Add the turmeric, salt, masala, potatoes, brinjals and dhania-jeero. Cook, covered, over a low heat for 20 minutes. Add the tomato and dhania leaves. Stir and cook for a further 10 minutes. (In Indian cuisine, do not add water to vegetables during cooking.)
**Time: 30 to 40 minutes**
**Serves 4 to 6**

# BRINJAL SLICES IN BATTER | *VENGRA IN BATTER*

*Serve this as a side dish with fish curry and rice, or as a starter with dhania chutney.*

2 large brinjals (aubergine/eggplant)
salt
cooking oil for frying

BATTER
375 ml (1½ cup) self-raising flour, sifted
3 ml (½ tsp) salt
3 ml (½ tsp) turmeric
10 ml (2 tsp) dhania-jeero (coriander-cumin)
15 ml (1 tbsp) dhania (coriander) leaves, chopped
5 ml (1 tsp) green masala
10 ml (2 tsp) cooking oil
250 ml (1 cup) cold water

Slice the brinjals lengthwise, 1 cm thick, but do not peel. Sprinkle them with salt until they weep, then pat dry. For the batter, combine the flour, salt, turmeric, dhania-jeero, dhania leaves, masala, oil and water (use enough water to form a thin batter). Heat some oil in a frying pan. Dip the brinjal slices in the batter then fry, turning once so that both sides cook until crisp. Remove and drain on absorbent paper. Serve immediately, with fresh tomato or chutney.
**Time: 20 minutes**
**Serves 4**

# FENUGREEK HERB & BRINJAL | *METHI NI BHAJI NA VENGAN*

*The fenugreek herb transforms any vegetarian dish into an Indian gourmet's delicacy, since the well-initiated acquire a taste for this bitter herb. Ideally, this dish should be served with a khitcheri and khudi (yellow rice and buttermilk gravy). Onion salad and a sweet lemon pickle also complement the bitter taste of this Gujerati dish. Fresh roti are a suitable accompaniment, but hot toast is also a good standby.*

300 g (3 bunches) methi (fenugreek) leaves
500 g brinjals (aubergine/eggplant)

VAGAAR
30 ml (2 tbsp) cooking oil
5 ml (1 tsp) jeero (cumin seeds)
3 ml (½ tsp) turmeric
10 ml (2 tsp) dhania-jeero (coriander-cumin)
3 ml (½ tsp) red masala
3 ml (½ tsp) salt

Cut away the roots and thick stems from the methi. Soak the leaves in cold water for 10 minutes, then rinse several times and chop finely.

Cut the brinjals into 2.5 cm squares, but do not peel.

To make the vagaar, heat the oil and jeero in a saucepan. Add the brinjals, turmeric, dhania-jeero and masala, followed by the methi leaves. Stir well, add salt, cover the saucepan and cook for 15 to 20 minutes over a medium heat.

**Time: 40 minutes**
**Serves 6**

# MUSHROOM & CASHEW NUT CURRY | *KAJU MAKHAN CURRY*

*For a creamy, rich and most delicious dish, try this curry. It imparts the delicate flavours of cashew nuts, saffron and cream which is a combination that never fails to impress even the uninitiated palate.*

45 ml (3 tbsp) ghee or oil
2 onions chopped
5 ml (1 tsp) garlic, pounded
5 ml (1 tsp) green masala or chopped green chilli
3 ml (½ tsp) turmeric
3 ml (½ tsp) salt
4 tomatoes, skinned and chopped or 30 ml (2 tbsp) tomato paste
500 g button mushrooms
100 g cashew nuts, crushed
a good pinch saffron strands
125 ml (½ cup) fresh cream or yoghurt
30 ml (2 tbsp) fresh dhania (coriander) leaves, chopped

Heat the ghee in a large, flat saucepan. Add the onions and fry until golden brown. Stir in the the garlic, masala, turmeric and salt, then fry for a few seconds. Add the tomatoes and cook, uncovered, until the sauce thickens and the extra moisture has evaporated.

Add the mushrooms, cashew nuts, saffron and cream. Stir well, cover and simmer for about 7 minutes over a low heat.

Garnish with dhania leaves and serve with hot roti or steamed basmati rice.
**Time: 40 minutes**
**Serves 4 to 6**

# SPINACH & MIXED VEGETABLE CURRY | *BHAJI NU SAKH*

*This vegetable curry is delicious on toast. Serve with khudi and khitcheri (yellow rice and buttermilk gravy).*

400 g (1 bunch) spinach, washed and
finely chopped
2 large onions, finely chopped
250 ml (1 cup) frozen mixed vegetables
or mixed vegetables, chopped
4 potatoes, diced
15 ml (1 tbsp) dhania-jeero
(coriander-cumin)
3 ml (½ tsp) turmeric
3 ml (½ tsp) salt
5 ml (1 tsp) green masala
10 ml (2 tsp) sugar

VAGAAR
125 ml (½ cup) cooking oil
5 ml (1 tsp) jeero (cumin seeds)
3 ml (½ tsp) rai (mustard seeds)

In a large dish, mix the spinach, onions, mixed vegetables, potatoes, dhania-jeero, turmeric, salt, masala and sugar. Toss well.

For the vagaar, heat the oil in a saucepan, then fry the jeero and rai for 10 seconds. Add the spinach mixture. Simmer, covered, for 20 minutes over a low heat or until the vegetables are soft.

**Time: 40 minutes**
**Serves: 6**

# STUFFED BABY BRINJALS | *BHARELA VENGAN*

*Indian baby brinjals have a delicate, sweet flavour, with a subtle bitterness in the skins (which are rich in vitamins). Serve the stuffed brinjals with roti, papadums and a pickle. There is an art to stuffing vegetables with the correct spices and ingredients. In this recipe, the coconut imparts a characteristic flavour.*

500 g baby brinjals (aubergine)

STUFFING
250 g fresh or frozen green peas
30 ml (2 tbsp) dhania (coriander) leaves, chopped
60 ml (4 tbsp) freshly grated coconut or 45 ml (3 tbsp) desiccated coconut
15 ml (1 tbsp) sugar
8 ml (1½ tsp) dhania-jeero (coriander-cumin)
5 ml (1 tsp) fresh ginger, pounded
3 ml (½ tsp) green masala or 1 chopped green chilli
3 ml (½ tsp) salt

VAGAAR
80 ml (⅓ cup) cooking oil
2 ml (¼ tsp) ground hing (asafoetida)

Wash the brinjals then pat dry with absorbent paper. Slit each brinjal lengthwise, twice, but only three-quarters of the way down. Season each with a pinch of salt.

Chop the peas coarsely in a food processor or mincer. Place them in a bowl with the dhania leaves, coconut, sugar, dhania-jeero, ginger, masala and salt. Mix this stuffing well and push a good quantity into each brinjal, using all the mixture.

To make the vagaar, heat the oil in a saucepan, sprinkle in the hing, then brown for 10 seconds. Gently arrange the brinjals and excess stuffing in the same saucepan and fry for about 3 minutes over a medium heat. Turn the brinjals over and cover the saucepan. Simmer for 20 minutes before serving.
**Time: 40 minutes**
**Serves 4**

# CUMIN POTATOES | *JEERA BATAKA*

*These cubed and spiced potatoes make a colourful side dish for roasts, as they are sprinkled with crushed jeero (cumin) and green dhania (coriander) leaves. If the potatoes are pre-boiled and kept at room temperature, the dish should take only 7 to 10 minutes to prepare.*

500 g potatoes
8 ml (1½ tsp) jeero (cumin seeds)
60 ml (4 tbsp) cooking oil
1 green chilli, sliced lengthwise
or 3 ml (½ tsp) green masala
5 ml (1 tsp) salt
10 ml (2 tsp) lemon juice
15 ml (1 tbsp) dhania (coriander) leaves, chopped

Boil the potatoes, then cut them into 12 mm cubes.

Dry roast the jeero in a pan for 2 minutes, then crush them finely with a rolling pin. Set aside.

Heat the oil in a large pan, add the chilli and brown for 5 seconds. Add the potatoes, salt and half the quanity of crushed jeero. Stir well, then fry for 3 minutes.

Serve immediately, garnished with the lemon juice, the remaining jeero and dhania leaves.

**Time: 40 minutes**
**Serves 2**

# SPECIAL MASHED POTATO | *VAGAARELI BATAKA*

*This spicy hot mashed potato is outstanding. Serve it with roasts.*

4 large potatoes
3 onions, sliced
2 dried red chillies
125 ml (½ cup) cooking oil
5 ml (1 tsp) salt
45 ml (3 tbsp) dhania (coriander) leaves, chopped

Boil and mash the potatoes.

Gently fry the onions and chillies in heated oil until soft. Remove the chillies. Stir in the salt and dhania leaves with the onions. Add the potatoes and stir well. Cover the pan and cook over a medium heat for 15 minutes. Crush the fried chillies and use them to garnish the potatoes before serving.

**Time: 45 minutes**
**Serves 4**

# HOMEMADE CHEESE IN SPINACH & PEAS | *BHAJI MATAR PANEER*

*This delicate vegetarian dish is one of India's specialities, with the homemade cheese (paneer) contributing a creamy texture and flavour. I serve paneer with hot roti, or better still, with alu roti and a crunchy onion kachoomer. Paneer may be prepared with various vegetables, but the spinach and peas combination is a favourite. You will need muslin or any clean, soft cloth to make the cheese.*

### PANEER
200 g frozen spinach (fine texture)
or 1 bunch fresh spinach
250 ml (1 cup) hot water
1 litre (4 cups) milk
30 ml (2 tbsp) lemon juice
30 ml (2 tbsp) melted ghee or butter
30 ml (2 tbsp) cooking oil
3 ml (½ tsp) rai (mustard seeds)
2 onions, chopped
3 ml (½ tsp) salt
3 ml (½ tsp) fresh ginger, pounded
3 ml (½ tsp) red masala
250 ml (1 cup) frozen peas

### GARNISH
15 ml (1 tbsp) dhania (coriander)
leaves, chopped

If using fresh spinach, simmer for 15 minutes in hot water, then purée.

Bring the milk to the boil in a saucepan. Add the lemon juice, then remove the saucepan from the heat. Stir until the whey separates. Line a muslin cloth in a colander and pour in the mixture. Tie the ends of the cloth to form a bag for the cheese. Allow the whey to run off and leave the bag to stand for 2 hours. Squeeze out any excess liquid by pressing. Cut the cheese into small cubes.

Gently fry the cheese cubes in ghee for 1 minute, then set aside.

Heat the oil in a saucepan. Add the rai and allow them to pop. Add the onions and fry for 3 minutes. Add the remaining spices, spinach and peas. Simmer, covered, for 20 minutes.

Add the cheese cubes and simmer for another 3 minutes. Garnish with the dhania leaves.

**Time: 40 minutes, plus 3 hours for cheese making**
**Serves 4**

Tie ends of cloth to form a bag for the cheese

Ready to hang the cheese bag

Cut the cheese into small cubes

# CAULIFLOWER & PEA CURRY | *PHOOLGOBI AUR MATAR KARI*

*This vegetable curry is served with hot roti or puri, or as a side dish with toover dhal and rice.*
*Sweet pickles or mango pickles are an appropriate accompaniment.*

1 cauliflower, washed and cut into
small pieces
500 ml (2 cups) frozen peas

1½ onions, chopped
2 small tomatoes, grated
5 ml (1 tsp) salt
5 ml (1 tsp) green masala
5 ml (1 tsp) turmeric

3 ml (½ tsp) fresh ginger, pounded

3 ml (½ tsp) fresh garlic, pounded
10 ml (2 tsp) dhania-jeero
(coriander-cumin)

VAGAAR
60 ml (4 tbsp) cooking oil or ghee
5 ml (1 tsp) jeero (cumin seeds)
5 ml (1 tsp) rai (mustard seeds)

GARNISH
30 ml (2 tbsp) dhania (coriander)
leaves, chopped

Mix the vegetables with the salt, masala, turmeric, ginger, garlic and dhania-jeero.

To make the vagaar, heat the oil in a large saucepan then brown the spices for 10 seconds. Add the vegetables, stir and cover. Cook over a low heat for 30 minutes.

Garnish with dhania leaves.

**Time: 45 minutes**
**Serves 6**

Daily fare: dhal (lentils), rice, cauliflower & peas, potato fry, raita and
sweet dried fruit pickle served with papadums on a banana leaf

# GREEN PEA CURRY | *VANTANA NU LEELU SAKH*

*This is a delicious green pea dish to serve with puffed puri or hot roti and a selection of pickles.*
*It may accompany any lamb dish. As a variation, omit the brinjal and tomato.*

500 ml (2 cups) frozen or fresh green peas
4 medium potatoes, diced
1 small brinjal (aubergine), diced but unpeeled
1 medium onion, finely chopped
3 ml (½ tsp) turmeric
3 ml (½ tsp) salt
10 ml (2 tsp) sugar
10 ml (2 tsp) dhania-jeero (coriander-cumin)
3 ml (½ tsp) green or red masala

VAGAAR
60 ml (4 tbsp) cooking oil and melted butter or ghee
3 ml (½ tsp) rai (mustard seeds)
2 tuj (cinnamon sticks), 5 cm each
5 ml (1 tsp) fresh ginger, pounded
250 ml (1 cup) warm water
1 small ripe tomato, diced (with skin)
30 ml (2 tbsp) dhania (coriander) leaves, chopped

Mix together the peas, potatoes, brinjal and onion in a large bowl. Add the turmeric, salt, sugar, dhania-jeero and masala, and mix with a spoon.

For the vagaar, heat the oil and butter or ghee to a high temperature. Quickly add the rai and tuj, then add the ginger and brown for 8 seconds. Mix this into the vegetable mixture, pour the water over and stir. Simmer, covered, in a saucepan over a medium heat for 15 to 20 minutes. Stir occasionally to prevent the vegetables from catching.

Add the tomato and dhania leaves and cook for another 10 minutes or until the tomato has absorbed the spices. Stir and serve.
**Time: 40 minutes**
**Serves 6**

# OVEN-BAKED POTATO WEDGES | *BATAKA*

6 potatoes
3 ml (½ tsp) salt
3 ml (½ tsp) black pepper
30 ml (2 tbsp) olive oil

Scrub the potatoes well, cut them into wedges but do not peel. Season with salt and pepper, then drizzle with the oil. Bake in an oven preheated to 180°C for 30 to 45 minutes until golden in colour.
**Time: 45 to 55 minutes**
**Serves 4**

# GOLDEN POTATOES | *TARELA BATAKA*

*Serve these golden-coloured potatoes with roasts, egg chops or fried fish.*

8 medium potatoes, peeled and halved
5 ml (1 tsp) salt
3 ml (½ tsp) turmeric
3 ml (½ tsp) green masala
60 ml (4 tbsp) flour for coating
125 ml (½ cup) ghee or oil

Mix the potatoes with the salt, turmeric and masala. Coat with flour.

Heat the ghee in a pan, add the potatoes, cover and cook for 20 minutes over a low heat. Remove the lid, increase the heat and sauté the potatoes until golden brown all over.
**Time: 30 to 40 minutes**
**Serves 6**

# MIXED VEGETABLE PIE | *GAAJAR MATAR LAGAN*

*Served with a fresh dhania or tomato chutney, this potato-topped vegetable pie goes particularly well with fried fish or chicken.*

### VEGETABLE FILLING
60 ml (4 tbsp) cooking oil or ghee
10 limri (curry leaves)
2 large onions, sliced
5 ml (1 tsp) fresh ginger, pounded
500 ml (2 cups) frozen peas
500 ml (2 cups) fresh or frozen diced carrots
3 ml (½ tsp) salt
3 ml (½ tsp) pepper
30 ml (2 tbsp) dhania (coriander) or mint leaves, chopped

### POTATO MASH
500 g potatoes, boiled soft
200 ml (½ cup) milk
3 ml (½ tsp) green masala
15 ml (1 tbsp) butter
5 ml (1 tsp) salt
2 ml (½ tsp) pepper

Prepare the vegetable filling while the potatoes boil. Heat the oil in a saucepan, then brown the limri for 10 seconds. Add the onions and ginger and fry for 5 minutes until soft. Stir in the vegetables, salt, pepper and dhania leaves. Cover and reduce the heat. Simmer for 20 minutes.

Mash the boiled potatoes to a smooth consistency, then mix in the milk, masala and butter. Season with salt and pepper. Beat with a fork until fluffy.

Place the vegetable filling in a pie dish and spread the mashed potatoes over the top. Use a fork to make wavy patterns. Bake the pie under a grill for 15 minutes, in the centre of the oven. To brown, raise the pie to the top shelf for a further 5 minutes.

**Time: 1½ hours**
**Serves 6**

# FRIED CABBAGE SPECIAL | *KHUBI FRY*

*This could be a main dish if served with puri, sweet pickles and papadums.*

500 g (½ medium) cabbage, thinly sliced
4 potatoes, cut into thin strips
3 onions, sliced
125 ml (½ cup) dhania (coriander) leaves, chopped
5 ml (1 tsp) green masala
8 ml (1½ tsp) salt
15 ml (3 tsp) dhania-jeero (coriander-cumin)
3 ml (½ tsp) turmeric
10 ml (2 tsp) sugar

VAGAAR
125 ml (½ cup) cooking oil
5 ml (1 tsp) rai (mustard seeds)
5 ml (1 tsp) jeero (cumin seeds)
5 ml (1 tsp) methi (fenugreek) seeds

Toss the cabbage and vegetables in a large dish with the spices, mixing well.

For the vagaar, heat the oil in a large saucepan with a well-fitting lid. Add the rai, jeero and methi, then stir in the cabbage mixture.

Maintain a high heat for the first 5 minutes. Keeping covered, reduce the heat to medium and cook for 15 minutes, tossing occasionally. Do not add water but allow the mixture to cook in its own liquid. By the end of the cooking time, the cabbage will reduce to half the original quantity, so do not be alarmed at the initial large quantity.

**Time: 30 minutes**
**Serves 4**

# Salads & side dishes

The best attribute of a salad is the glamour it lends any table. Eye appeal is important and depends largely on the crispness of the ingredients; the greens and other hues of an uncooked salad are bright and deep. Raw vegetables are rich in vitamins and minerals. Use a selection of fresh lettuce, carrots, beetroot, celery and cherry tomatoes. Soak them for a short while in cold water to preserve the vitamins.

Freshen up a salad by spraying it with cold water. Jazz up the flavour with a dressing of orange or lemon juice, a drizzle of olive oil and a squirt of balsamic vinegar.

### Raitas and kachoomers

Indian salads are well seasoned and dressed. A raita has a yoghurt base, usually spiced with freshly roasted jeero, black peppercorns and chopped chillies. A kachoomer is based on chopped or diced purple Indian onions which are crunchy and sweet, unlike the strong ones available in South Africa. Chopped tomatoes and green peppers (capsicum) are added and the whole seasoned with spices, malt vinegar and salt.

### Chutneys and pickles

Fresh herbs form the base of many of the chutneys that accompany Indian meals. The celebrated Indian herb, dhania (coriander), takes pride of place, followed by mint, green onions, tomatoes, apples, coconut and dates. All are blended into an exquisite thick chutney or sambal.

Pickles are also indispensable in an Indian menu. Mangoes, lemons, limes, dried fruit, carrots and a variety of freshly picked vegetables are only some of the popular pickles concocted.

Since they are usually hot, pickles are intended for veteran food lovers. As Indian food is, rightly, only moderately spiced, it is the role of the various pickles to add extra heat for those who seek hot Indian food.

### Papadums

Papadums or papads are served with many dishes. They are sun-dried lentil or rice flour discs that may be stored for use at any time. Papadums may be grilled or fried.

# PAPADUMS | *PAPADS*

*Known as papads in the East, papadums are a perfect accompaniment to vegetarian meals. Tempered with the correct balance of chillies and spices, the wafer-thin crips will enhance a delicately spiced meal. As preparation is time consuming, many leave this task to the perfectionists in India who export delicious papads to the rest of the world. To make your own, use a thali, a stainless steel or aluminium tray, on which to roll the papads. Choose a hot summer's day for making papads, as they need sun and the dough needs to stand overnight.*

500 g urad lentil flour, or rice
or cake flour
8 ml (1½ tsp) salt
8 ml (1½ tsp) bicarbonate of soda
25 ml (5 tsp) red chilli powder
or 3 fresh green chillies, finely pounded
a pinch ground hing (asafoetida)
2 ml (½ tsp) jeero (cumin seeds),
crushed
200 ml (½ cup) water
10 ml (2 tsp) cooking oil

Sift the dry ingredients and bind to a stiff dough with the water. Leave overnight.

Coat the dough with the oil (to prevent stickiness), then push it through a mincer 3 times to create a fine texture.

Knead thoroughly to a soft, pliable dough and divide into small walnut-sized balls. Roll each ball on the back of a thali, forming a very thin disc. Gently place on a cloth in direct sunlight. Leave for at least 8 hours in direct sunlight to dry out until they are crisp. (Make sure the wind does not blow them away!)

**Time: approx. 2 hours (depending on cooking method), plus 8 hours drying**
**Makes 50**

## TO STORE

Stored uncooked in an airtight container (papads last almost indefinitely). Cooked papads may be stored in a plastic bag in an airtight tin for 2 to 3 days.

## DEEP FRYING

Deep fry papads in hot oil for 5 seconds. Use two forks to lift them out after 5 to 8 seconds. Drain and serve immediately. (Exposure to air will soften a papad after a few hours.)

## GRILLING

Papads may be cooked under a hot oven grill for 10 seconds, or on a wire rack over an electric plate. Rotate them quickly and turn over, as they burn easily. Grill for about 15 seconds on either side (the 'wet' look must disappear). A light brown papad is required. Papads become crispy as they cool.

# CUCUMBER RELISH | *KHAKADI RAITA*

*This refreshing relish complements any menu. It makes a delicious dip as well.*

500 ml (2 cups) thick yoghurt (or 250 g cream cheese)
1 large English cucumber
3 ml (½ tsp) salt
5 ml (1 tsp) ground jeero (cumin seeds)
2 ml (½ tsp) green masala
2 ml (½ tsp) prepared mustard or
3 ml (½ tsp) ground rai (mustard seeds)

Line a colander with a clean, fine muslin cloth. Pour the yoghurt onto the cloth and tie a knot. Leave to hang, undisturbed, for a while until all the moisture has dripped away, leaving behind a thick cheese.
(If using the cream cheese, follow the same method but hang only for about 30 minutes.)

Grate the cucumber, but do not peel. However, if using another variety, peel first and deseed. Squeeze out the moisture and leave to dry in a cloth.

Mix all the ingredients well and chill in the refrigerator. Serve chilled, with vegetarian dishes. It is particularly good with rice and lentils.

**Time: 1 hour, plus extra time for cheese-making**
**Serves 4**

Carrot raita, cucumber relish, kachoomer
with paapri and papadums

# CUCUMBER FINGERS | *KHAKADI*

*This hot relish is served with khudi and khitcheri (yellow rice with buttermilk gravy) and vegetarian dishes.*

1 medium cucumber (any variety)
3 ml (½ tsp) salt
3 ml (½ tsp) green masala or chopped green chilli
30 ml (2 tbsp) dhania (coriander) leaves, chopped

Peel the cucumber, then slice into 12 mm thick fingers. Rub the salt, masala and dhania leaves onto the cucumber and serve.
**Time: 10 minutes**
**Serves 6**

### VARIATION FOR CUCUMBER DAHI

Pour 1½ cups buttermilk over the spiced cucumbers (as prepared in the recipe above), then garnish with a sprig of dhania herb. This is excellent with biryani. When chilled, it also makes a deliciously cool summer salad.

# STEAMED BRINJALS WITH YOGHURT | *VENGRA KA RAITA*

*This raita is a very refreshing way of serving brinjals. Served chilled, it is soothing and cooling, especially with 'hot' vegetable dishes.*

500 g brinjals (aubergine)
500 ml (2 cups) yoghurt or buttermilk
3 ml (½ tsp) freshly ground black pepper
3 ml (½ tsp) chilli powder
5 ml (1 tsp) salt
30 ml (2 tbsp) whole mint or dhania (coriander) leaves

Peel the brinjals and cut into 2.5 cm squares. Steam them for 4 minutes until soft.
Mix together the yoghurt, spices and brinjals in a deep bowl. Decorate with mint or dhania leaves.
**Time: 15 minutes**
**Serves 6**

# FRESH TOMATO & ONION SALAD | *KACHOOMER*

*Kachoomers are the traditional Indian salads served with meat, chicken or fish dishes.*

2 large onions, sliced
1 large tomato, sliced
3 ml (½ tsp) jeero (cumin seeds)
10 ml (2 tsp) salt
5 ml (1 tsp) sugar
10 ml (2 tsp) lemon juice
30 ml (2 tbsp) vinegar
15 ml (1 tbsp) dhania (coriander) leaves, chopped

Toss the ingredients in a salad bowl. Garnish with dhania leaves.
**Time: 10 minutes**
**Serves 4**

# CARROT RAITA | *GAJAAR RAITA*

1 large carrot
250 ml (1 cup) yoghurt
30 ml (2 tbsp) green pepper, chopped
5 ml (1 tsp) jeero (cumin seeds), crushed
3 ml (½ tsp) salt

Peel and grate the carrot finely. Place the yoghurt in a bowl, then mix in the carrot, green pepper, jeero and salt. Stir well and chill.
    Serve with any biryani or rice dish.
**Time: 30 minutes**
**Serves 4**

# BEETROOT & ONION SALAD | *KANDA KACHOOMER*

*This crunchy beetroot salad complements Khubi Gosht Tarkhari. If you use pickled beetroot, halve the quantity of vinegar.*

1 bunch beetroot
2 onions, sliced
5 ml (1 tsp) salt
20 ml (4 tsp) sugar
125 ml (½ cup) brown vinegar
60 ml (4 tbsp) cold water
sprigs dhania (coriander) to garnish

Cook the beetroot for approximately 45 minutes, then peel and slice. Mix them with the onions in a large bowl. Add the salt, sugar, vinegar and water and mix well. Garnish with the dhania.
**Time: 1 hour**
**Serves 4**

# Sauces

## Garlic-Chilli Sauce

*Pour this tangy sweet-and-sour dressing over fried rice or tossed salads, or use as a dip for freshly fried chilli bites, or with chicken in batter.*

60 ml (4 tbsp) cooking oil
125 ml (½ cup) water
30 ml (2 tbsp) sugar
125 ml (½ cup) white vinegar
5 ml (1 tsp) fresh garlic, pounded
5 ml (1 tsp) green masala
5 ml (1 tsp) salt

Place all the ingredients in a mixing bowl and beat with a rotary beater until well blended. Bottle and store in the refrigerator.
**Time: 10 minutes**
**Serves 4**

## Hot Red Chilli Sauce

*This fiery sauce is for chilli lovers. Serve it with any dish that requires chilli heat.*

15 ml (1 tbsp) cooking oil
5 ml (1 tsp) rai (mustard seeds)
40 g tamarind
200 ml (³/₄ cup) water or 45 ml (3 tbsp) lemon juice mixed with 125 ml (½ cup) water
10 ml (2 tsp) red chilli powder
5 ml (1 tsp) salt
5 ml (1 tsp) fresh garlic, pounded
60 ml (4 tbsp) brown vinegar
15 ml (1 tbsp) cooking oil
5 ml (1 tsp) rai (mustard seeds)

Soak the tamarind in the water for 15 minutes. Loosen the seeds from the soaked pulp. Strain, but retain the liquid.
Mix the chilli powder, salt, garlic and vinegar with the tamarind liquid.
Heat the oil in a saucepan, add the rai and allow to pop.
Stir in the tamarind pulp.
Cool and bottle.
**Time: 15 minutes**
**Serves 4**

Garlic-chilli sauce, hot red chilli sauce and spiced buttermilk drink

# Fresh Chutneys & Pickles

## PEANUT CHUTNEY | *SHINGH CHUTNEY*

*Smoothly ground peanuts make a tasty chutney. Serve this one with savouries or main dishes.*

200 ml (½ cup) roasted peanuts
3 ml (½ tsp) green masala
5 ml (1 tsp) fresh garlic, pounded
5 ml (1 tsp) salt
125 ml (½ cup) brown vinegar
45 ml (3 tbsp) lemon juice
100 g (1 bunch) dhania (coriander) herb, roots removed
45 ml (3 tbsp) fresh mint, chopped (optional)

Chop the peanuts in a food processor until fine. Add the remaining ingredients and blend until smooth.
**Time: 15 minutes**
**Serves 6**

## CURRY LEAF TOMATO CHUTNEY | *LIMRI CHUTNEY*

*This refreshing chutney may be served with any Indian dish, but it is particularly good with fish.*

2 large ripe tomatoes, cut into wedges
20 fresh limri (curry leaves) (use dried if fresh unavailable)
juice of ½ lemon
3 ml (½ tsp) salt
3 ml (½ tsp) green masala
2 ml (½ tsp) fresh garlic, pounded
10 ml (2 tsp) sugar

Blend all the ingredients in a food processor, until well reduced to a smooth consistency.
**Time: 10 minutes**
**Serves 4**

# TOMATO CHUTNEY | *TAMATI CHUTNEY*

*Put a dollop of this tasty tomato chutney over roast potatoes, or as a complement to mince kebaabs, samoosas or savoury baked dishes.*

2 large red tomatoes, grated
5 ml (1 tsp) jeero (cumin seeds), crushed
5 ml (1 tsp) chopped green chilli or
green masala
5 ml (1 tsp) dhania (coriander)
leaves, chopped
5 ml (1 tsp) lemon juice
5 ml (1 tsp) brown vinegar
2 ml (¼ tsp) salt

Mix all the ingredients well together in bowl.
**Time: 10 minutes**
**Serves 4**

# FRESH COCONUT CHUTNEY | *NARIYAL CHUTNEY*

*This tangy, southern Indian fresh chutney is traditionally made from the beautiful coconuts grown in the region. Spread a layer of the chutney over hot dosa, the lentil pancakes enjoyed at breakfast time.*

flesh of ½ fresh coconut
2 to 3 green chillies
5 ml (1 tsp) fresh ginger, pounded
30 ml (2 tbsp) sugar or ghor
30 g tamarind
80 ml (⅓ cup) water
3 ml (½ tsp) salt
125 ml (½ cup) water

Soak the tamarind in the water for 15 minutes. Strain, then add the juice to the rest of the ingredients in a food processor, mincer or liquidiser. Reduce to a fine paste.
**Time: 20 minutes**
**Serves 4**

# FRESH MANGO CHUTNEY | *CHUNDO*

*This sweet mango chutney is typical of the State of Gujerat, the land of my forefathers, where a sweet taste highlights many dishes, including mango chutneys and pickles.*

500 g fresh mangoes, peeled and stoned
10 ml (2 tsp) salt
2 ml (½ tsp) turmeric
125 ml (½ cup) sugar
15 ml (1 tbsp) red chilli powder (use half for a milder chutney)
10 ml (2 tsp) jeero (cumin seeds), crushed
3 ml (½ tsp) fresh garlic, pounded
45 ml (3 tbsp) water

Place all the ingredients into a blender or food processor and reduce to a purée. Store in the refrigerator.
**Time: 15 minutes**
**Serves 6**

# APPLE & MINT CHUTNEY | *APPLE POODINI CHUTNEY*

*This outstanding fresh chutney is easy to prepare. Its refreshing apple taste complements meat or chicken very well, particularly tandoori chicken or roast lamb.*

1 large apple, peeled
250 ml (1 cup) fresh mint leaves
10 ml (2 tsp) jeero (cumin seeds)
5 ml (1 tsp) salt
3 ml (½ tsp) fresh garlic, pounded
5 ml (1 tsp) green masala
5 ml (1 tsp) lemon juice
10 ml (2 tsp) sugar

Slice the apples. Wash the mint well.
   Place all the ingredients in a food processor or liquidiser and blend to a thick pureé.
**Time: 10 minutes**
**Serves 6**

# CORIANDER CHUTNEY | *DHANIA CHUTNEY*

*Coriander is the celebrated basic ingredient of so many Indian dishes. Its distinctive flavour is highlighted in this chutney, possibly the most popular chutney in Indian cuisine. It is an essential accompaniment for mince kebaabs and goes well with samoosas and savouries.*

100 g (1 bunch) dhania (coriander) leaves
1 tomato, cut into wedges
5 ml (1 tsp) jeero (cumin seeds)
3 ml (½ tsp) salt
3 ml (½ tsp) green masala
3 ml (½ tsp) fresh garlic, pounded
15 ml (1 tbsp) lemon juice
15 ml (1 tbsp) brown vinegar

Remove the roots from the dhania, then rinse thoroughly in cold water.

Place all ingredients in a liquidiser or food processor and reduce to a pureé. Serve fresh, although dhania chutney may be stored in a refrigerator for 4 to 5 days.
**Time: 15 minutes**
**Serves 6**

VARIATION FOR MINT CHUTNEY
Use 1 cup fresh mint leaves in place of the dhania.

VARIATION FOR CORIANDER-PEANUT CHUTNEY
Add ½ cup salted peanuts to the Coriander Chutney. Mix in a liquidiser until smooth with a creamy, peanut texture.

# SALTED GREEN MANGO PICKLE | *MITHI KERI*

1 kg tender green mangoes
1 kg salt
4 green chillies (optional)

Wash the mangoes, then pat dry with absorbent paper. If the mangoes are large, slice them into quarters (small mangoes may be left whole). Using a sterilised jar with a well-fitting lid, arrange the salt and mangoes in alternate layers. Close the lid securely. Shake the bottle twice daily for 30 days.
**Time: 30 minutes, plus 30 days standing**
**Makes 1 kg**

# fRESH GREEN MANGO pICKLE | *TAJI KERI NA ATANA*

*Buy the variety of mango used for eating, not the very small, green pickle mangoes.*

I large green mango, cut into small pieces
3 ml (1/2 tsp) salt
30 ml (2 tbsp) cooking oil
5 ml (1 tsp) pickle masala
5 ml (1 tsp) garlic, pounded
a pinch turmeric
30 ml (2 tbsp) sugar

VAGAAR
15 ml (1 tbsp) cooking oil
6 limri (curry leaves)
3 ml (½ tsp) rai (mustard seeds)
3 (½ tsp) methi (fenugreek) seeds

Sprinkle the mango pieces with the salt and leave overnight. The following day, drain the excess liquid.

Heat the oil in a saucepan, then add the masala, garlic, turmeric, sugar and the mango. Cook for 15 minutes or until very soft.

For the vagaar, heat the oil in a pot, then add the limri, rai and methi. Finally, add the mango mixture and stir well. Leave to cool and store in the refrigerator.

**Time: overnight, plus 30 minutes**
**Serves 4**

# SWEET LEMON pICKLE | *LIMOO NA ATANA*

*This is a simple lemon pickle to make when lemons are plentiful. Packed in presentation bottles, lemon pickle makes an ideal gift.*

2 kg large lemons
100 g salt
8 ml (1½ tsp) chilli powder
15 ml (1 tbsp) turmeric
15 ml (1 tbsp) ground hing (asafoetida)
500 g sugar or ghor

Wash and cut each of the lemons into eight pieces. Add the remaining ingredients to the lemons. Mix well and store in a sterilised jar.

Stir the pickles every day for 30 days, by which time the lemons will be soft and ready to eat.

**Time: 30 minutes**
**Makes 2 kg**

# SWEET CARROT PICKLE | *MITHI GAAJAR NA ATANA*

*This crisp, sweet carrot pickle is easy to prepare and adds colour to any table.*

8 medium carrots
30 ml (2 tbsp) sugar
15 ml (1 tbsp) golden syrup
5 ml (1 tsp) salt

3 ml (½ tsp) fresh garlic, pounded
10 ml (2 tsp) chilli powder
4 tuj (cinnamon sticks), 4 cm
each (optional)
80 ml (⅓ cup) cooking oil

3 ml (½ tsp) turmeric
80 ml (⅓ cup) brown vinegar
sprigs mint or dhania (coriander)
to garnish

Peel and slice the carrots lengthwise into thin sticks. Mix them in a large dish with the remaining ingredients, except the garnish.

Garnish with the mint sprigs and serve immediately. It may be stored for up to 2 weeks in the refrigerator, but will lose its crispness after a while.

**Time: 20 minutes**
**Serves 6**

# KUMQUAT PICKLE | *KUMQUAT ATANA*

*This tiny, pungent, citrus fruit makes an ideal pickle to serve with vegetarian dishes.*

250 g kumquats
5 ml (1 tsp) chilli powder
5 ml (1 tsp) salt
15 ml (1 tbsp) golden syrup
125 ml (½ cup) cooking oil
3 ml (½ tsp) turmeric

Wash and halve the kumquats. Squeeze out any excess liquid. Mix them with the remaining ingredients and store in a sterilised glass jar.

**Time: 30 minutes**
**Makes 250 g**

# MANGO PICKLE | *KERI NA ATANA*

*The masala or spice mixture for this traditional pickle may also be used to spice fresh vegetables such as carrots, cauliflower, onions, cucumbers or beans, which are then served as fresh pickles.*

2 kg green mangoes
500 ml (2 cups) salt
200 g ground methi (fenugreek) seeds
100 g mustard seeds
60 ml (4 tbsp) chilli powder
45 ml (3 tbsp) turmeric
15 ml (1 tbsp) ground hing (asafoetida)
250 ml (1 cup) cooking oil for mixing
750 ml (3 cups) cooking oil for pickling

Wipe the mangoes with a wet cloth and cut each into 8 pieces lengthwise. Arrange them in a large dish.

Make a spice mixture with the salt, methi, mustard seeds, chilli powder, turmeric and hing. Add 1 cup oil and mix well into the spices. Rub the mixture over the mango pieces. Transfer the mangoes to a sterilised jar and seal well.

After two days, pour the mangoes into a bowl and cover them completely with 3 cup oil. Leave the pickle to stand (covered in the bowl) for 4 weeks before serving.

**Time: 1½ hours**
**Makes 2 kg**

### VARIATION
Slice the mangoes into 4, lengthwise, but keep the base intact. Stuff them with the spice mixture and continue as above.

# VEGETABLE PICKLE | *BHAJI NA ATANA*

*Serve this pickle in small quantities with lentil dishes.*

1 kg fresh vegetables (eg. green beans, green peppers (capsicum), cauliflower, peas and carrots)
2 ml (¼ tsp) bicarbonate of soda
6 green chillies, sliced lengthwise
250 ml (1 cup) cooking oil
8 ml (1½ tsp) salt
30 ml (2 tbsp) mustard powder
10 ml (2 tsp) chilli powder
5 ml (1 tsp) turmeric
375 ml (1½ cups) brown vinegar
30 ml (2 tbsp) cornflour

Wash, then cut the vegetables into bite-sized pieces. Place them in a saucepan and cover with warm water. Bring to the boil, then add bicarbonate of soda and boil for a further 3 minutes. Drain the vegetables in a colander and leave to stand overnight.

Dry the vegetables well the following day, then place in a dish. Mix in the chillies, oil, salt, mustard and chilli powders, and turmeric.

In a small pot, combine the vinegar and cornflour into a paste. Bring it to the boil over a medium heat then, stirring all the time, simmer for 10 minutes until a thick mass forms. Pour the mixture over the vegetables and mix well until the vegetables are well coated. Leave to cool, then bottle and store.

**Time: 1 hour, plus overnight drying**
**Makes 750 g**

# SWEET DRIED FRUIT PICKLE | *MITHI ATANA*

*This exceptional yet easy sweet pickle never fails to impress guests. Serve it with any menu.*

250 g mixed dried fruit
60 ml (4 tbsp) brown vinegar
8 ml (1½ tsp) mustard powder
8 ml (1½ tsp) chilli powder
60 ml (4 tbsp) cooking oil
5 ml (1 tsp) turmeric
5 ml (1 tsp) salt
5 ml (1 tsp) fresh garlic, pounded
45 ml (3 tbsp) sugar
5 ml (1 tsp) lavang (whole cloves)
4 tuj (cinnamon sticks), 5 cm each
8 ml (1½ tsp) whole black peppercorns
45 ml (3 tbsp) golden syrup

Wipe the fruit with a damp cloth, then slice each piece of fruit into strips about 6 mm thick. Arrange in a large bowl.

Mix the vinegar in a cup with the mustard and chilli powders. Pour over the fruit. Add the remaining ingredients. Mix well and store in a sterilised jar. Leave to stand for 3 to 4 days.
**Time: 30 minutes**
**Makes 250 g**

Sweet mango slices

Salted green mango pickle

green grapes covered with pickle masala

Lemon pickle

Sweet dried fruit pickle

Vegetable pickle

# Desserts & Sweetmeats

*As with any work of art, the making of sweetmeats is extremely time consuming. The Indian housewife invariably buys her sweetmeats from one of the many confectioners who are only too willing to sell their homemade 'mithai'. The jostling streets beside railway stations are lined with vendors selling an infinite variety.*

*Even the tiniest villages in India boast more than a dozen sweet vendors, leaving me rather envious because I have to do my sweetmaking at home.*

On my travels through India, I discovered that sweets are eaten there in many different ways. As I moved from the west towards Gujerat in the north (the birthplace of my parents), it became evident from the custom of offering a sweet as a first course, that the average Indian possesses an unparalleled sweet tooth! A sweet first course would invariably be accompanied by a fried puri or bread of some kind. Surprising as it may seem, Indians believe that sweets increase the appetite, rather than diminishing it.

The Bengalis in eastern India surpass every other community when it comes to sweet eating, often enjoying sweet courses as their entire meal content. Bengal is famous for a particular type of sweetmeat, which is soft and pure white: the outstanding rasgoolla, whose immortality in India is assured. Prominent among the sweets of the subcontinent, rasgoolla is the Indian answer to French crêpes suzette, Italian zabaglione, the American baked Alaska, or South African melktert.

Rasgoolla has even been rhapsodised by the great Indian poet, Rabindranath Tagore. Legend has it that one, Nabin Chandra Das of North Calcutta was inspired to invent rasgoolla in the early 19th century. This master created small, soft balls of unsalted cottage cheese and boiled them in a thick sugar syrup until they achieved just the right combination of succulence and sponginess to cause them to emit a tiny squeak when bitten. What a delightful thought! Legend goes on to assert that Nabin Chandra Das's nephew, Keshab Chandra Das, added to the family tree of sweets when he created rasmalai, a second cousin to rasgoolla, served in a creamy syrup.

I have a sneaking suspicion that my over-indulgence in gaajar halwa (that Punjabi culinary triumph of a carrot pudding based on ghee and nuts) may have caused my Indian hosts in Delhi some embarrassment. It was there that I partook of my first family meal in India.

My successful and hospitable host and hostess and their 13-year-old daughter, who was bubbling over at having finally reached teenagehood, seated me beside them on the floor. We sat on a beautiful Kashmir carpet and ate from a communal platter; hot roti were brought in one at a time by the hostess. Her cook had obviously mastered the technique of producing perfectly round, puffed-up roti, because each looked like a work of art.

At last, the final course arrived, that exquisite sweet, warm carrot halwa topped with pistachio nuts and served in individual bowls. I remember thinking that this sweet could only have been prepared by one of the expert confectioners who line the streets of Delhi. Delhi was cool that night and the warm, rich halwa was just wonderful, making it difficult to resist my third helping.

Later, my Indian pride swelled when I found that the dessert had been prepared by none other than the 13-year-old daughter. I was so thrilled that the traditional custom of teaching a young Indian girl the basic know-how of cooking has not been lost in India after all.

India's festive sweets command their own special place in Eastern cuisine. Diwali is the most prominent Hindu festival of the year. As the festival of lights, it signifies the triumph of good over evil, and millions of little clay lamps are lit all over the villages, towns and cities of India on the eve of Diwali. For this auspicious festival a special range of exotic sweetmeats are prepared a week or two in advance.

Milky burfi laden with edible pure silver, pistachios, almonds and exotic nuts is a highlight of Diwali. Burfi holds the key to that secret alchemy that transmutes mere sweetness into a memorable confection. Just as there is a special way to savour a glass of vintage claret, so there is a way to eat burfi: take a small bite and allow the piece to melt gradually on the tongue, imparting all the subtlety of its flavour as it slowly dissolves.

I believe burfi was primarily invented for children, however, of all Indian sweets it is totally irresistible and my personal favourite–even though it is extravagantly calorific.

Other mouth-watering festive sweetmeats, such as jalebis, ladu and pak, are usually included in an Indian bride's gift, traditionally given to her by the groom's family to symbolise a sweet relationship.

# RICH MILK SWEETMEAT | *BURFI*

*A North Indian delicacy, Burfi mithai reigns supreme on the list of sweetmeats, especially when decorated with edible pure silver paper. Burfi is a thick layer of reduced milk, blended with almonds, ghee and syrup. The fine-textured sweetmeat is placed aside for 24 hours to set, becoming a moist, melt-in-the-mouth sweetmeat with a tantalising richness. Patience is needed to produce burfi; do not be discouraged by the perfection it demands.*

*The edible silver leaf is optional, as it is purely for decoration, but does add a touch of class and a sense of celebration. Using food colouring, colour half the almonds for garnishing green and the other half yellow. For a single serving, two 4 cm squares of burfi should be quite adequate, as the sweetmeat is very rich.*

### MILK MIXTURE
2 litres (8 cups) milk
80 ml (1/3 cup) lemon juice
500 g milk powder

### SYRUP
500 ml (2 cups) sugar
500 ml (2 cups) water
a few drops rose essence

### FINAL STAGE
200 ml (3/4 cup) ghee
45 ml (3 tbsp) almonds, chopped
25 ml (5 tsp) elachi (cardamom) seeds
(removed from pods, roasted in pan for
1 minute and crushed)
10 ml (2 tsp) grated jaiphul (nutmeg)
3 strips pure silver leaf (optional)

In a heavy saucepan, bring the milk to the boil over a medium heat. Stir occasionally, as the milk tends to catch on the bottom and burns easily. Simmer for 1 hour.

Remove from the heat and stir in the lemon juice; the milk should curdle immediately. Pour the curdled milk into a colander and allow the whey to separate out; the curds will remain in the colander. Discard the whey. Leave to cool.

Combine the milk curds with the milk powder in a large bowl and stir well. Using the fine side of a grater, grate the milk mixture, then set these fine-textured lumps aside. (A large sieve may also be used, but pressing the lumps through takes longer this way.)

In a large, heavy saucepan (approximately 24 cm in diameter), bring the sugar and water to the boil over high heat. Keep boiling for 15 minutes, then add the essence. Test the syrup by placing a drop on a saucer. If it forms a small crystal ball immediately, the syrup is ready. If not, boil the syrup for a further 5 minutes. (The secret of making perfect burfi lies in the correct consistency of the syrup.)

Add the milk mixture to the syrup and stir to a smooth texture. Keep over a medium heat and gently stir in the ghee, about 2 tbsp at a time. Add half the quantity of almonds and elachi seeds, plus all the jaiphul. Simmer, still over a medium heat, for 45 minutes and stir occasionally. When the mixture has lost its stickiness and does not adhere to the side of the saucepan when stirred, it is ready. Remove from the heat.

While the milk and syrup mixture simmers, colour the remaining almonds with food colouring.

Pour the mixture into a large, greased glass ovenproof dish about 30 cm square, or into two smaller dishes. (Do not use a metal baking tray.) Sprinkle with the coloured almonds and elachi seeds, and decorate with the silver leaf if using. Leave for 24 hours to set. Cut into 4 cm squares and store in an airtight container in the refrigerator.

**Time: 2 hours, plus 1 day to set**
**Makes 750 g**

# MILK SWEETMEAT | *SIMPLE BURFI*

### MILK MIXTURE
500 g milk powder
180 ml (²/₃ cup) canned cream
30 ml (2 tbsp) ghee
20 ml (4 tsp) crushed elachi
(cardamom) seeds
10 ml (2 t ) grated jaiphul (nutmeg)
30 ml (2 tbsp) chopped almonds
30 ml (2 tbsp) chopped pistachio nuts

### SYRUP
500 ml (2 cups) water
500 ml (2 cups) sugar
a few threads kesar (saffron)

In a deep bowl, mix together the milk powder, cream and ghee with your fingertips until the mixture has a fine texture.

Stir in the elachi and jaiphul. Add half the almonds and pistachios into the mixture. Set aside.

For the syrup, bring the water to the boil in a saucepan, then add the sugar. Stir and allow to boil until the syrup thickens to a 'drop' consistency. Add the kesar, which imparts a slightly yellow shade.

Stir in the milk mixture until smooth, thick and creamy. Remove and leave to cool. Pour into a small, greased dish until the burfi is about 25 mm in height. Garnish with the remaining almonds and pistachios. Top with a few more threads of kesar.

Leave to set for a day, then cut into 4 cm squares. Store in the refrigerator.
**Time: 1 hour, plus 1 day to set**
**Makes 500 g**

# PRETZEL-SHAPED SWEETS | *JALEBI*

*In the Indian state of Uttar Pradesh, jalebi are often eaten with milk for breakfast. This brilliantly coloured sweet is one of the most popular Indian sweetmeats, particularly on festive occasions. You will need an icing bag with a plain nozzle (5 mm in diameter), but a funnel or an empty condensed milk tin with a hole punctured in the bottom will suffice.*

### BATTER
500 ml (2 cups) cake flour
15 ml (1 tbsp) rice flour (optional)
2 ml (½ tsp) baking powder
450 ml (1½ cups) warm water
750 ml (3 cups) cooking oil for deep
frying

### SYRUP
500 ml (2 cups) sugar
2 ml (³/₄ tsp) cream of tartar
450 ml (1½ cups) cold water
3 ml (½ tsp) jalebi colouring or yellow
food colouring
30 ml (2 tbsp) rose water

Festive sweetmeats: jalebi, burfi,
halwa, naan khataai

In a bowl, sift together the cake flour, rice flour and baking powder. Mix to a smooth, thick consistency with the warm water. Set the batter aside for 5 days  (leave it unsealed out of the refrigerator).

Combine the sugar and cream of tartar with the cold water in a saucepan. Stir over a medium heat until the sugar dissolves. Increase the heat to high and boil the syrup rapidly for 5 minutes. Remove from the heat and add the colouring and rose water. Keep the syrup warm.

To make the jalebis, heat the oil in a deep frying pan. Spoon the batter into an icing bag and squeeze directly onto the hot oil, looping a stream of batter to and fro five or six times to form a pretzel-shaped spiral. Each jalebi should be about 6 cm in diameter.

Fry in batches of 5 or 6 until golden brown (about 1 minute either side). Remove and place immediately in the warm syrup for 1 minute, then drain on a wire rack.
**Time: 1 hour, plus 5 days standing**
**Makes 500 g**

# MILK CHEESE BALLS IN SYRUP | *RASGOOLLA*

*Bengal is famous for this sweetmeat. Even though making rasgoolla is a lengthy process and the sweet is extravagantly rich in calories, I find it totally irresistible.*

### CHEESE
1 litre (4 cups) milk
20 ml (4 tsp) lemon juice
15 ml (1 tbsp) cake flour or semolina
3 ml (1½ tsp) baking powder

### SYRUP
250 ml (1 cup) sugar
1 litre (4 cups) water
a few drops rose or vanilla essence

To make the cheese, bring the milk to the boil in a saucepan. Stir in the lemon juice. Remove from the heat and leave to stand for 15 minutes. The milk should curdle, creating a clean whey.

Pour off the whey into a muslin cloth or bag and tie. Suspend the bag until the rest of the whey has drained out. (This takes up to 4 hours.) The cheese left behind should be completely dry and solid. A weight may be placed on the muslin bag if all the whey has not drained out.

Remove the cheese from the cloth and knead to a soft paste with the flour and baking powder. Roll the paste into balls the size of large marbles.

Boil the sugar, water and essence in a saucepan for 15 to 20 minutes. When the syrup is slightly sticky and begins to bubble, gently lower the cheeseballs into the saucepan. Cover, then cook over low heat for 15 minutes, turning the balls over repeatedly. Remove the lid and swing the saucepan with a circular movement, then cover again. Repeat for about 45 minutes until the balls are soft and spongy. (They will remain white.)

Serve warm in small bowls with the syrup.
**Time: 2 hours, plus 4 hours for cheese to dry**
**Serves 3 to 4**

### VARIATION: RASMALAI
Serve the cheese balls cold in a cream made by boiling 2 litres milk until reduced to half the quantity. Flavour with ½ C sugar, 1 t crushed elachi (cardamom) seeds and 1 t rose essence.

# CRUSHED WHEAT SWEET | *LAAPSI*

*This Gujerati pudding has an unusually coarse texture, flavoured with tuj (cinnamon), elachi (cardamom) and soomph (aniseed). It is served warm as a first course for vegetarian meals, but makes a satisfactory dessert in any menu.*

125 ml (½ cup) melted ghee
250 ml (1 cup) laapsi (crushed wheat)
2 tuj (cinnamon sticks), 4 cm each
15 ml (1 tbsp) slivered almonds
5 ml (1 tsp) elachi (cardamom) seeds, crushed
5 ml (1 tsp) large soomph (aniseed), crushed
500 ml (2 cups) boiling water
125 ml (½ cup) sugar

Heat the ghee in a heavy saucepan with a well-fitting lid. Add the crushed wheat and toss for 3 to 5 minutes, or until the wheat turns golden brown. Stir in the tuj, almonds, elachi and soomph.

Add the water, cover and cook over a medium heat for 30 minutes or until the wheat is soft, then add the sugar, cover and cook for another 10 minutes.

Serve warm. If the sweet is to be reheated, add ⚘ C water and warm over a low heat, stirring it up with a fork.

**Time: 40 minutes**
**Serves 4**

# BENGALI DELIGHTS | *GOOL GOOLAS*

*These golden, fried balls from Bengal are a winner with children. Dipped in syrup, they have a delicious aniseed flavour.*

375 ml (1½ cups) self-raising flour
80 ml (⅓ cup) sugar
1 egg, beaten
10 ml (2 tsp) large soomph (aniseed), roasted 1 minute in pan and crushed
125 ml (½ cup) milk
750 ml (3 cups) cooking oil for frying

SYRUP
500 ml (2 cups) sugar
500 ml (2 cups) water
3 ml (½ tsp) vanilla essence

Sift the flour into a bowl. Add the sugar, egg and soomph, then bind into a soft batter with the milk. Leave to stand for 30 minutes.

To make the syrup, boil the sugar and water together for about 15 minutes. Remove from the heat, add the vanilla essence and keep warm.

Heat the oil in a deep frying pan. Drop the batter into the oil (about ½ tbsp at a time) to form balls the size of a walnut. Fry about 10 goolas at a time over a medium heat until golden brown. Remove and dip into the warm syrup for 30 seconds.

Serve warm in individual bowls, with a spoonful of leftover syrup poured over each.

**Time: 30 minutes, plus 30 minutes standing**
**Serves 4 to 6**

# WARM CARROT DESSERT | *GAAJAR HALWA*

*Standing out boldly on vegetable stalls in India are heaps of stout and bright red carrots. (Quite unlike the variety familiar to us, Indian carrots are far sweeter and more vividly coloured.)*

*The luscious carrot halwa that I relished in India was an experience to remember. In this Punjabi dessert, the carrots blend beautifully with the nutty flavour of almond and pistachios gently cooked in butter, cream and milk, creating an unusual and easy dessert that never fails to impress. I serve it warm in cut-glass bowls, dressed with a generous helping of cream and topped with extra pistachios. It may also be served as a cold sweet. Carrot halwa takes time to prepare, but you can safely continue with other tasks while it simmers away. It may be prepared several days in advance and reheated gently. It also freezes well.*

750 g carrots
100 g butter or ghee
30 ml (2 tbsp) slivered almonds
200 ml (½ cup) sugar (or less, to taste)
250 ml (1 cup) milk
125 ml (½ cup) fresh cream
8 ml (1½ tsp) elachi (cardamom) seeds, crushed
30 ml (2 tbsp) pistachio nuts, finely chopped
250 ml (1 cup) fresh cream, whipped

Peel the carrots and grate them finely (preferably in a food processor).

Melt the butter in a heavy saucepan, add the almonds and toss for 1 minute. Add the carrots and stir for about 10 minutes over a higher heat.

Stir in the sugar, milk and ½ cup cream with a wooden spoon. Simmer, uncovered, over a medium heat for 20 minutes until all the moisture evaporates. Mix in the elachi and half the pistachios. Simmer for 10 minutes, stirring occasionally with a fork to separate the carrot shreds. The halwa should be soft and moist. Don't be alarmed; the quantity of carrots will reduce as the moisture evaporates.

Serve warm in individual bowls and decorate with the remaining pistachios and the whipped cream.

**Time: 1 hour 10 minutes**
**Serves 4**

Warm carrot dessert served with saffron icecream

# BENGALI SWEETMEATS | *GOOLAB JAMUNS*

*My children love Goolab jamuns with desiccated coconut sprinkled liberally over them as they are removed from the syrup.*

750 ml (3 cups) cake flour
13 ml (2½ tsp) baking powder
500 ml (2 cups) cream of wheat or semolina
90 ml (6 tbsp) ghee
15 ml (1 tbsp) cooking oil
15 ml (1 tbsp) ground jaiphul (nutmeg)
10 ml (2 tsp) elachi (cardamom) seeds (heated in pan for 30 seconds, then finely crushed)
1 x 397 g can condensed milk
250 ml (1 cup) lukewarm water

SYRUP
900 g sugar
750 ml (3 cups) water
3 ml (½ tsp) lemon juice
10 ml (2 tsp) rose water or a few drops vanilla essence

FOR FRYING
250 ml (1 cup) melted ghee
750 ml (3 cups) sunflower oil

In a deep bowl, sift together the flour and baking powder. Add the cream of wheat, ghee, oil, jaiphul and elachi and rub to a fine texture with your fingertips. Add the condensed milk and bind to a soft dough with the lukewarm water. Knead well for about 1 minute.

Take approximately ½ tbsp dough and press into an oval between your palms. Roll into a cigar shape, about 6 x 1 cm. Repeat until all the dough is used.

To make the syrup, boil the sugar and water together for 15 to 20 minutes. Flavour with the lemon juice and rose water, then remove from the heat before it becomes sticky. The syrup must be thin. Keep warm.

In a deep pan or saucepan, heat the melted ghee and oil to a medium temperature. Gently slide in about 10 goolab jamuns and fry slowly until they turn pale brown; they will expand and split at the centre. Remove them from the oil and dip immediately into the warm syrup for about 10 seconds. Drain in a colander.

Store in an airtight container.

**Time: 1 to 1½ hours**
**Makes 1 kg**

# SWEET COTTAGE CHEESE DESSERT | *EASY SEEKHUND*

*This cooling, Gujerati dessert resembles thick cream and is delicately flavoured with almonds, jaiphul (nutmeg) and elachi (cardamom). The smooth texture is complemented by the pastry-like fried puri that are served with seekhund. Although seekhund is traditionally made from the homemade cheese called paneer, this is an easy alternative.*

2 x 250 g cartons cottage cheese or cream cheese
125 ml (½ cup) sugar
10 ml (2 tsp) ground jaiphul (nutmeg)
5 ml (1 tsp) elachi (cardamom) seeds, lightly crushed
250 ml (1 cup) fresh cream
10 ml (2 tsp) almonds, chopped

In a blender, whip together the cheese, sugar, jaiphul and elachi for 2 to 3 minutes until smooth. Transfer to a bowl.

Whisk the cream with an eggbeater until it thickens, then fold it into the cheese mixture, mixing well with a wooden spoon.

Scoop the mixture into individual bowls and garnish with the almonds. Children may prefer a garnish of colourful hundreds and thousands, or chocolate vermicelli. Serve with fried puri.

**Time: 15 minutes**
**Serves 6**

### VARIATION
Mix in fresh fruit of your choice, and sprinkle with a few kesar (saffron) threads.

# SWEET CHEESE DESSERT | *SEEKHUND*

2 litres thick sour milk
250 ml (1 cup) fresh cream
200 g cream cheese
250 ml (1 cup) castor sugar
5 ml (1 tsp) elachi (cardamom) seeds, crushed
5 ml (1 tsp) ground jaiphul (nutmeg)
15 ml (1 tbsp) pistachio nuts, finely sliced
15 ml (1 tbsp) slivered almonds
5 ml (1 tsp) threads kesar (saffron), heated in a saucepan and finely crushed

Line a fine muslin cloth in a colander. Pour in the sour milk and tie a knot to form a bag. Suspend the bag for 1 to 1½ days, after which the cheese will be fairly dry.

In a large bowl, beat the fresh cream until stiff and thick. Add the home-made cheese, cream cheese and castor sugar, then stir well. (This could be blended in a food processor to make it light and fluffy.) Add the elachi and jaiphul, then fold in the whipped cream.

Scoop into an attractive glass bowl. Decorate with the nuts and sprinkle with the kesar. Serve with puris.

**Time: 1 day (to make cheese), plus 30 minutes**
**Serves 6**

# WARM MILK PUDDING | *DOODH PAK*

*This delicious, warm, milk pudding is thickened with rice and flavoured with nuts.*

4 litres (16 cups) milk
30 ml (2 tbsp) basmati or white long-grain rice
125 ml (½ cup) sugar
10 ml (2 tsp) ground elachi (cardamom)
15 ml (1 tbsp) charoli (chirongee) nuts
15 ml (1 tbsp) almonds, sliced lengthwise

In a heavy, deep saucepan, bring the milk to the boil. Add the rice and simmer for 1 hour over a medium heat, stirring occasionally.

Add the sugar, elachi and nuts, then simmer for a further 20 minutes. As the rice softens, the milk will thicken to a creamy consistency.

Serve warm in individual bowls, with pieces of puri.

**Time: 1½ hours**
**Serves 6**

# QUICK & EASY MILK DESSERT | *EASY DOODH PAK*

1 litre milk
410 g can evaporated milk
80 ml (⅓ cup) vermicelli
125 ml (½ cup) sugar
10 ml (2 tsp) ground elachi (cardamom)
15 ml (1 tbsp) charoli (chirongee) nuts
15 ml (1 tbsp) almonds, sliced lengthwise

Follow the method as for Warm Milk Pudding (above), but simmer for half the time.
**Time: 40 minutes**
**Serves 4**

# CREAMY MILK SWEET | *BASUNDI*

*Basundi has the consistency of cream and is traditionally eaten in Gujerat as a rich first course for a vegetarian meal.*

4 litres (16 cups) milk
5 ml (1 tsp) lemon juice
200 ml (¾ cup) sugar
15 ml (1 tbsp) elachi (cardamom) seeds, crushed
10 ml (2 tsp) almonds, chopped
15 ml (1 tbsp) charoli (chirongee) nuts

Boil the milk rapidly in a heavy saucepan, stirring frequently so that the milk does not catch. After 30 to 40 minutes the milk should thicken and reduce to half its quantity.

Pour in the lemon juice and stir. The milk will become granular. Add the sugar and elachi, and stir. Pour into individual bowls and garnish with the nuts. Serve hot or cold, with fried puri.

**Time: 1½ hours**
**Serves 4 to 6**

# RICH CARDAMOM BISCUITS | *NAAN KHATAAI*

*These tasty biscuits are festive fare: small rounds topped with almonds or tiny silver balls.*

250 ml (1 cup) ghee or soft butter
250 ml (1 cup) sugar
250 ml (1 cup) chana flour
750 ml (3 cups) cake flour
5 ml (1 tsp) baking powder
15 ml (1 tbsp) elachi (cardamom) seeds, crushed
6 almonds, cut into strips
10 ml (2 tsp) silver balls

Cream together the ghee and sugar. In another bowl, sift all the flour and baking powder together. Add the elachi.

Mix the flour mixture into the ghee and sugar to form a soft dough. Knead well for 15 minutes until the dough is pliable.

Preheat the oven to 180°C. Shape small balls of dough into disks with a 2 cm diameter. Flatten slightly and decorate half the batch with pieces of almonds, the other half with silver balls.

Place on a greased baking tray and bake in the centre of the oven for 10 to 12 minutes until light brown.

Store in an airtight tin.

**Time: 1 hour**
**Makes 50**

# SPICED MANGO PULP | *KERI NAU RUS*

*This Gujerati sweet consists of fresh mango pulp served chilled. Each diner spices his or her own portion and eats the rus by dipping pieces of fried puri into it from a central platter.*

4 ripe Alphonse mangoes
125 ml (½ cup) milk
5 ml (1 tsp) salt
10 ml (2 tsp) sugar (optional)

SEASONINGS
30 ml (2 tbsp) white pepper
30 ml (2 tbsp) ground ginger
30 ml (2 tbsp) jeero (cumin seeds), roasted and finely crushed

Peel the mangoes and cut the flesh away from the pip. Place in a blender or liquidiser with the milk and salt. (Add sugar if you prefer extra sweetness.) The traditional Indian method for this dessert involves squeezing the mangoes between the palms of the hand.

Chill the mango pulp in a bowl. Serve with pepper, ginger and jeero, and a standard quantity of puri.

**Time: 30 minutes**
**Serves 4 to 6**

# ALMOND & NUT SWEETMEAT | *BADAMI HALWA*

*This brightly coloured sweetmeat consists of almonds and other nuts set in a base of kesar (saffron)*
*syrup thickened with sago and ghee.*

125 ml (½ cup) sago
500 ml (2 cups) cold water
800 g sugar
300 ml water
10 ml (2 tsp) lemon juice
125 ml (½ cup) cornflour
900 ml water
3 ml (½ tsp) red and 3 ml (½ tsp) yellow colouring or
5 ml (1 tsp) green colouring
125 ml (½ cup) ghee, solidified
150 g blanched almonds, split
30 g pistachio nuts
30 g charoli (chirongee) nuts (optional)
1 whole jaiphul (nutmeg), grated
10 ml (2 tsp) elachi (cardamom) seeds, crushed
2 ml (½ tsp) threads kesar (saffron)

Soak the sago in the 2 cups water for 30 minutes, then drain.

Dissolve the sugar in the 300 ml water in a large, heavy saucepan. Add the lemon juice, bring to the boil and boil for 15 minutes. Do not stir.

Dissolve the cornflour in the 900 ml water and add to the syrup with the sago and colouring. Cook, stirring continually, for 1 hour.

Stir in the ghee 1 tbsp at a time, mixing well with each addition. Cook for another 45 minutes. (By this time the halwa should come away from the sides of the saucepan without sticking.)

Add the nuts, jaiphul, elachi and kesar to the halwa and stir. Cook for 15 minutes. Pour into a greased dish (20 cm square) and leave to set for 12 hours. Cut into 4 cm squares.

**Time: 2½ hours, plus 12 hours setting**
**Makes 2 kg**

TO STORE
Wrap in foil and store in an airtight container for 4 to 6 weeks.

# SWEET VERMICELLI | *MITTHI SEV*

*Despite its Gujerati origin, I like to serve this warm sweet in a non-traditional way-with freshly whipped cream and a squeeze of lemon juice.*

60 ml (4 tbsp) extra fine vermicelli
15 ml (1 tbsp) sultanas
125 ml (½ cup) melted ghee
250 ml (1 cup) warm water
125 ml (½ cup) sugar
3 ml (½ tsp) ground jaiphul (nutmeg)
5 ml (1 tsp) elachi (cardamom) seeds, crushed
10 ml (2 tsp) slivered almonds

In a saucepan, add the vermicelli and sultanas to the ghee and toss over a medium heat until the vermicelli is golden. Reduce the heat to low, add the water, cover and cook for about 10 minutes, or until the vermicelli is soft.

Add the sugar, jaiphul and elachi and cook for another 10 minutes. Sprinkle with almonds and serve warm in individual bowls.

**Time: 30 minutes**
**Serves 4**

# MILK DESSERT | *PHIRNI KASHMIRI*

45 ml (3 tbsp) rice
250 ml (1 cup) water
5 ml (1 tsp) kesar (saffron)
30 ml (2 tbsp) hot milk
500 ml (2 cups) milk
60 ml (4 tbsp) sugar
60 ml (4 tbsp) mixed nuts (almonds, pistachios, charoli, cashews)
5 ml (1 tsp) elachi (cardamom) seeds, crushed

Soak the rice in the water for 30 minutes, then drain. While the rice is soaking, soak the kesar in the hot milk for 15 minutes.

Pour the 2 cups milk in a saucepan. Add the rice, sugar and half the nuts. Bring to the boil, then simmer for 35 minutes. The milk will reduce to a thick consistency. Remove from the heat.

Add the kesar milk and simmer for 10 minutes. Reduce to a smooth texture in a blender. Dish into individual bowls and garnish with elachi and the remaining nuts. Chill before serving.

**Time: 1 hour**
**Serves 2 to 3**

# SAFFRON ICECREAM | *KESAR KHULFI*

*Khulfi wallahs, India's icecream makers, are famous for their imaginative flair in concocting icecreams. Tropical fruits such as mangoes, pawpaws, bananas or lychees, and Eastern flavourings such as kesar (saffron), rose petals and elachi (cardamom) elevate Indian icecream into an exotic creation. The icecream is made with reduced milk, rather than cream.*

15 ml (1 tbsp) cornflour
60 ml (4 tbsp) milk
3 ml (½ tsp) kesar (saffron)
30 ml (2 tbsp) milk
750 ml (3 cups) milk
397 g can condensed milk
2 ml (¼ tsp) vanilla essence
125 ml (½ cup) fresh cream

Mix the cornflour and 4 tbsp milk into a paste.

Heat the kesar in a dry pan, then soak in 2 tbsp milk.

Combine the 3 cups milk and condensed milk in a heavy saucepan. Blend in the cornflour paste and bring to the boil, stirring occasionally, as the milk tends to catch. Add the kesar milk and vanilla essence and simmer for 15 minutes. Remove from the heat and leave to cool.

Pour the mixture into ice trays and freeze until semi-set. Remove from the ice trays and whisk well. Blend in the cream, stir and pour into a large container for freezing. Allow to freeze for 4 to 6 hours, or until solid.

**Time: 45 minutes, plus 4 to 6 hours freezing**
**Serves 4**

# MANGO ICECREAM | *KERI KHULFI*

*This southern Indian mango icecream surpasses all others in taste, quality and originality.*

1½ litres (6 cups) milk
2 egg yolks
125 ml (½ cup) sugar
3 mangoes, peeled and pulped in blender
125 ml (½ cup) fresh cream, whipped until fluffy

Boil the milk in a heavy saucepan for 30 minutes, stirring occasionally until the milk reduces to three-quarters of its original volume.

Beat the egg yolks and sugar, then add gradually to the warm milk. Stir and simmer for 25 minutes until the milk thickens. Set aside to cool completely.

Add the mango pulp, stir and freeze in a flat container until semi-set. Remove from the freezer and whip until fluffy. Blend in the whipped cream and freeze for 4 to 6 hours, or until solid.

**Time: 1 hour, plus 4 to 6 hours freezing**
**Serves 4**

# CREAM of WHEAT PUDDING | *SOJI* (*SHEERO*)

*Soji is food fit for the gods-one of the chief offerings of prasadum (holy food) in Hindu temples. On a vegetarian menu, this traditional sweet should be the first course, particularly for weddings or on festive occasions. Roasting the wheat over a very slow heat will emphasise the delicate aroma and colour of this warm sweet dish from Gujerat. For a vegetarian meal, try it as a starter to tickle the taste buds and enhance the appetite.*

250 ml (1 cup) ghee
250 ml (1 cup) cream of wheat or semolina
15 ml (1 tbsp) sultanas
15 ml (1 tbsp) almonds, sliced lengthwise
375 ml (1½ cups) warm water
250 ml (1 cup) warm milk
250 ml (1 cup) sugar
5 ml (1 tsp) ground jaiphul (nutmeg)
5 ml (1 tsp) elachi (cardamom) seeds, crushed

Heat the ghee in a saucepan over a medium heat. Reduce the heat, then add the cream of wheat, sultanas and almonds and toss very slowly for at least 15 minutes or until the semolina becomes slightly pink. The sultanas will swell when heated.

Add the water and milk, then cover and cook slowly for 20 mintues. Stir in the sugar and seasonings. Cover, switch off the heat and leave for 10 to 12 minutes. The resulting texture should be grainy.

Fluff up the mixture with a fork and serve warm.
**Time: 20 minutes**
**Serves 4**

# INDIAN BEVERAGES

## SPICED TEA | DESI CHAI

*Tea is extremely popular in India, particularly Darjeeling tea from Assam. The leaves are boiled with milk and water, then flavoured with a spiced tea masala, consisting of spices such as elachi (cardamom), pepper and tuj (cinnamon). A pinch of freshly ground pepper will do just as well. Fragrant citronella grass and fresh ginger add a characteristic Indian flavour.*

375 ml (1½ cups) water
250 ml (1 cup) milk
12 mm piece fresh ginger, pounded
2 ml (½ tsp) tea masala (see below) or a pinch freshly ground pepper
2 elachi (cardamom pods), partly split
1 blade citronella grass, cut into pieces (optional)
8 ml (1½ tsp) tea leaves
20 ml (4 tsp) sugar

Bring the water and milk to the boil in a deep saucepan. Do not allow it to boil over. Add the ginger, tea masala, elachi and citronella grass. Simmer gently over medium heat for 3 minutes.

Add the tea leaves and stir in the sugar. Bring to the boil and simmer for a few minutes until the tea mixture turns a caramel colour.

Remove from the heat and strain into a teapot. In Indian homes, tea is poured in the kitchen before being served to guests.
**Time: 10 minutes**
**Serves 2**

Desi chai - Indian tea served with naan khataay

# ROSE MILK DRINK | *fALOODA*

15 ml (1 tbsp) tukmaria seeds (available from Indian stores)
250 ml (1 cup) cold water
1 litre (4 cups) milk
60 ml (4 tbsp) white sugar
15 ml (1 tbsp) rose essence
15 ml (1 tbsp) rose syrup (add more for a deeper colour)

Soak the tukmaria seeds in the water for 20 minutes. Strain and set the enlarged seeds aside.

Place the remaining ingredients into a blender, with the seeds. Blend well. (A hind whisk may be used as an alternative.)

To serve, pour the falooda into 4 tall glasses. If you like, add a scoop of vanilla ice cream to each glass and decorate with pale pink rose petals.

**Time: 30 minutes**
**Serves 4**

Rose milk and seekhund with small bowls of sugar-coated aniseed, slivers of betel nut and salted sesame seeds

## THE END OF AN INDIAN MEAL

At the very end of an Indian meal, paan is offered as an aid to digestion—a highly necessary finale! Paan comprises a firm green betel leaf wrapped around a piece of betel nut and a variety of interesting goodies: aniseed, coloured coconut, lime paste, cardamom seeds and, for the connoisseur, tobacco. The betel leaf is folded neatly into a triangle and secured with a clove. Paan temporarily stains the lips red but refreshes the mouth.

Paan wallahs, who make and sell paan, are found on almost every street in India, as paan is chewed between and after meals. In Varanasi (Benares) on the holy river Ganjas, the paan wallahs are kept especially busy by the thousands of pilgrims who visit the temples of this ancient city. In one of the tiny shops lining the narrow streets - some are barely 1.5 m wide and the sun never reaches them - I was arrested by the sight of huge glass bottles filled with ingredients for paan: aniseed coated with brightly coloured sugar, rose perfumes, betel nut slivers, and edible pure silver leaf. I ordered a mixture to bring back to South Africa, and an extra helping of aniseed was offered to me as a traditional farewell by the charming old shopkeeper, who was clad only in a loin cloth.

Since paan is not easily available in South Africa, you could instead serve aniseed as an after-dinner refresher: roast 100 g of aniseed (see instructions for roasting spices), place on a small plate and offer to your guests.

# DINING THE EASTERN WAY

Indian food is traditionally served on a polished circular metal tray. Each person is given a large tray called a thal and a smaller one called a thali. The various foods are placed on the thali, as well as earthenware bowls or katori containing chutneys and lentil soup. In southern India large banana leaves are used in place of the thali. The convenience of such disposable plates would appeal to many of us today.

In rural India, it is still common practice to sit cross-legged on the floor for meals. Cutlery is an unnecessary commodity, since eating with your fingers is the only way to savour Indian food. No true Indian feels happy about eating with a knife and fork. It is simply impossible to enjoy a hot roti with cutlery. All this may sound messy, but even little children soon learn to handle rice in a very neat manner.

Traditional etiquette requires only the right hand to be used in eating, as the left hand is considered unclean.

Hands are washed both before and after meals. Northern Indians are particularly fussy about how food is eaten, never allowing food past the first knuckle. Southern Indians are far less inhibited and will plunge the whole hand into their food.

A traditional order of precedence is maintained in the serving of meals. Men and guests are served first, children next and women last. To a Westerner, this may seem a slight, but Indians regard it as a gracious gesture for a woman to serve the men of her family first; the act in fact denotes a dignified disposition rather than being a sign of subordination.

My concept of a contemporary formal dinner party is to serve each dish of a three or four course menu separately, so that each aroma, taste and experience may be enjoyed to the very last mouthful. Time is needed, the whole idea being to savour the delightful experience of these exotic dishes your hostess has taken hours to prepare.

The concept of serving an Indian meal in courses is not new. However, the second course of a traditional Indian meal may be too varied and overwhelming, so I suggest serving the dishes separately.

At a vegetarian meal, a warm sweet is traditionally served first. This surprising custom, prevalent among the Gujerati community, springs from the belief that sweets stimulate the appetite. In a non-vegetarian menu, the first course might consist of a savoury such as samoosas with chutney, followed by a selection of dishes such as dhal, vegetables, hot roti, fresh salads, pickles, papadums and a meat dish richly cooked in gravy. The final course would be a sweet such as khulfi (a creamy ice cream), fruit, or one of the syrupy sweets made with homemade cheese.

Selecting the right dishes is vital in ensuring the success of a menu. Avoid dishes that look and taste similar. Colour and texture are both important factors to bear in mind. Nothing is more boring for a guest than food haphazardly placed on the table, especially if the guests cannot tell one dish from the next.

All Indian meals may be planned and prepared in advance, leaving the hostess time to ensure that her table is elegantly set. Flowers scattered on the table, soft candlelight and brightly coloured table linen, in either reds or blues, are most attractive for a special Indian dinner. For an authentic touch, try seating guests on the floor on comfortable cushions, around a low table. Every hostess should strive to express her own personality in the way she offers food to her guests. Remember, too, that a good hostess is not only judged by her food, but by her manner.

# Glossary

| | | | |
|---|---|---|---|
| **Aamli** | Tamarind | **Diwali** | Hindu festival of lights |
| **Adoo** | Root ginger | **Doodh** | Milk |
| **Ajmo** | Ajowan seeds, also known as ajwain | **Dora mari** | White peppercorns |
| **Ajowan** | see Ajmo | **Dosa** | Pancakes of rice and lentil flour |
| **Ajwain** | see Ajmo | **Elachi** | Cardamom pods or seeds |
| **Arad** | Turmeric, also known as halud | **Foodino** | see Poodini |
| **Atana** | Pickles | **Foolka** | Fried yeast bread |
| **Ayurveda** | Ancient Hindu treatise on medicine | **Gaajar** | Carrot |
| **Basmati rice** | Long-grain Indian rice | **Gharum** | |
| **Basundi** | Gujerati milk dessert, eaten as a first course in a vegetarian meal | **masala** | A hot garnish of mixed ground spices |
| | | **Ghor** | Indian molasses crystals, also called sugar jaggery |
| **Bataka** | Potatoes | | |
| **Beja** | Sheep's brains | **Ghor papdi** | Sweetmeat made with sugar jaggery |
| **Bhaji** | Vegetable or herb | **Goolab** | |
| **Bhajia** | Chilli bites | **jamuns** | Bengali sweetmeat |
| **Bhinda** | Okra or ladyfingers (vegetable) | **Goal goolas** | Bengali sweetmeat |
| **Biryani** | Rice dish with lentils and a base of meat, fish or vegetables | **Gosht** | Meat |
| | | **Green masala** | Pounded green chilli, ginger and garlic paste |
| **Bombay duck** | Dried species of Indian fish | | |
| **Boomla** | Bombay duck | **Halud** | Turmeric, also known as arad |
| **Boti** | Pieces of meat | **Halwa** | Sweet or pudding |
| **Burfi** | Indian sweetmeat | **Handi** | Indian pots |
| **Chaat** | Indian snacks | **Hing** | Asafoetida, a powerful flavouring |
| **Chai** | Indian spiced tea | **Idli** | Southern Indian rice cakes served with a gravy called sambar |
| **Chakki** | Stone discs for grinding wheat and spices | | |
| | | **Inda** | Egg |
| **Chana** | Chickpea | **Jaggery** | Indian molasses crystals (see Ghor) |
| **Chana dhal** | Split chickpea | **Jaiphul** | Nutmeg |
| **Chapati** | Unleavened bread, also called roti | **Jalebi** | Pretzel-shaped Indian sweetmeat |
| **Charoli** | Indian nuts, also known as chirongee | **Jinga** | Prawns |
| **Chasni** | Syrup | **Kabuli chana** | Whole chickpea |
| **Chaval** | Rice | **Kachoomer** | Salad with onion base |
| **Chevra** | Savoury noodle mix | **Kaddu** | Courgettes |
| **Chirongee** | see Charoli | **Kaleji** | Liver |
| **Chori bean** | Dried Indian bean | **Kanda** | Onions |
| **Citronella grass** | Aromatic for flavouring Indian tea | **Kara mari** | Black peppercorns |
| **Dahi** | Spiced buttermilk drink | **Karahai** | Deep pan resembling a wok |
| **Dhal** | Lentils, or a thick lentil purée | **Karchi** | Ladle |
| **Dhania** | Coriander herb or seeds | **Karela** | Bitter Indian gourd |
| **Dhania-jeero** | Mixed powder of ground coriander and cumin seed | **Kari** | Gravy |
| | | **Kariyapula** | Curry leaves, also called limri |

| | | | |
|---|---|---|---|
| **Katori** | Bowl used for chutney and soup | | mung beans |
| **Kebaab** | Mince balls | **Moong dhal** | Split yellow lentils, also called maghni dhal |
| **Kekda** | Crab | **Moorkhoo** | Savoury fried noodles |
| **Kera** | Banana | **Mugh** | *see Moong* |
| **Keri** | Mango | **Murghi** | Chicken |
| **Kesar** | Saffron | **Naan** | Round oven-baked bread |
| **Khakadi** | Cucumber | **Nariyal** | Coconut |
| **Khima** | Minced meat | **Oil lentils** | Lentils known as toover dhal |
| **Khitcheri** | Yellow lentil rice, served with the gravy called khudi | **Okra** | Ladyfingers, a vegetable known as Karela in India |
| **Khopra** | Fresh coconut kernel | **Paan** | Green betel leaf with filling, chewed after meals to refresh the mouth |
| **Khubi** | Cabbage | | |
| **Khudi** | Warm buttermilk gravy served with khitcheri | **Paapri** | Fried lentil savoury |
| **Khulfi** | Indian icecream | **Paaya** | Sheep's trotters |
| **Khumbi** | Mushrooms | **Paneer** | Homemade Indian cheese |
| **Kofta** | Savoury vegetable balls | **Papadi** | Indian green beans |
| **Korma** | Meat in a yoghurt gravy | **Papads** | Sun-dried lentil flour discs, also called papadums |
| **Laapsi** | Crushed wheat Gujerati pudding | | |
| **Lagan** | Pie or baked dish | **Papadums** | *see Papads* |
| **Lahsan** | Garlic | **Paratha** | Flaky unleavened bread |
| **Lal masala** | Pounded red chilli, ginger and garlic paste | **Patra** | Leaf |
| | | **Phirni** | Kashmiri milk pudding |
| **Lassi** | Indian drink of spiced yoghurt or buttermilk | **Phoolgobi** | Cauliflower |
| | | **Pilau** | Flavoured rice |
| **Lavang** | Cloves | **Poodini** | Mint, also called foodino |
| **Leelo masala** | Pounded green chilli, ginger and garlic paste | **Poora** | Spiced pancakes |
| | | **Prasad** | Food offered to the gods in a temple |
| **Limri** | Curry leaves | **Pur** | Paper-thin pastry for samoosas |
| **Lombhia** | Black-eyed beans | **Puri** | Puffed deep-fried bread |
| **Machi** | Fish | **Rai** | Mustard seeds |
| **Madumbi** | A root vegetable with broad leaves | **Raima beans** | Red kidney beans |
| **Masala** | Mixture of ground spices and flavourings | **Raita** | Yoghurt-based relish or side dish |
| | | **Rasgoolla** | Indian dessert or sweetmeat |
| **Masoor dhal** | Brown lentils | **Rasmalai** | Variation of rasgoolla |
| **Masoor ni dhal** | Split pink lentils | **Red masala** | Paste of red chilli, ginger and garlic |
| | | **Rose essence** | Flavouring |
| **Matar** | Peas | **Rose syrup** | Red syrup flavoured with rose essence |
| **Matka** | Earthenware water pot | | |
| **Methi** | Fenugreek seeds | **Roti** | Unleavened bread, also called chapati, cooked on a griddle |
| **Methi bhaji** | Fenugreek herb | | |
| **Mircha** | Chilli | **Rubari** | Sindhi milk pudding |
| **Mithai** | Sweetmeat | **Saffron** | Stigmas of the crocus flower |
| **Moong** | Green lentils, also called mugh or | **Sambar** | Lentil gravy served with the rice |

| | |
|---|---|
| | cakes called idli |
| **Samoosa** | Triangular deep-fried pastry with spiced meat or vegetable filling |
| **Seekh** | Steel skewers for outdoor grilling |
| **Sev** | Fine lentil-flour noodles |
| **Shaas** | *see* Dahi, as usually referred to as dahi |
| **Shingh** | Peanuts |
| **Silver leaf** | Pure silver edible paper, used for elaborate decoration, usually on sweetmeats |
| **Sitaphal** | Custard apple |
| **Soji** | Gujerati cream of wheat pudding, served as a first course in a vegetarian meal |
| **Soomph** | Large aniseed |
| **Tal** | Sesame seeds |
| **Tamarind** | Pods soaked to produce the sweet-sour flavouring, tamarind water |
| **Tamati** | Tomato |
| **Tandoor** | Cylindrical clay oven used for the tandoori method of cooking |
| **Tandoori** | *see* Tandoor |

| | |
|---|---|
| **Tapela** | Flat Indian pots, also called handi |
| **Tarkhari** | Meat or chicken cooked in a spiced gravy |
| **Tavi** | Griddle for cooking roti, also known as a tawa |
| **Tawa** | *see* Tavi |
| **Tea masala** | Spice mixture for flavouring Indian tea |
| **Thali** | Stainless steel trays for dining |
| **Tikka, tikkie** | Patty, small cake |
| **Toover dhal** | Oil lentils, also known as tur dhal |
| **Tur dhal** | *see* Toover dhal |
| **Tuj** | Cinnamon/cassia |
| **Urad dhal** | Black gram (lentils) |
| **Vaal ni dhal** | Split Indian bean |
| **Vagaar** | Tempering of spices in hot oil, to release their aroma for a dish |
| **Varyari** | Large aniseed |
| **Vedas** | Ancient Hindu scriptures |
| **Vehlan** | Indian rolling pin |
| **Vengan** | Brinjal (aubergine) |
| **Vengra** | Brinjal (aubergine) |

# INDEX

*Indian recipe names are italicised; all recipe names have an initial capital letter*